INTEGRATING NATURE-BASED SOLUTIONS FOR CLIMATE CHANGE ADAPTATION AND DISASTER RISK MANAGEMENT

A PRACTITIONER'S GUIDE

John Matthews and Ernesto Ocampo Dela Cruz

JUNE 2022

ASIAN DEVELOPMENT BANK

Contents

Tables, Figures, and Boxes

TABLES

FIGURES

BOXES

Acknowledgments

This publication is a knowledge product of the Asian Development Bank (ADB) under the regional knowledge and support technical assistance program, Protecting and Investing in Natural Capital in Asia and the Pacific (TA 9461-REG).

It is based on the implementing consultant's report prepared by John Matthews and Ernesto Ocampo Dela Cruz. The final manuscript was developed by a team led by Isao Endo (environment specialist, Environment Thematic Group) and Qingfeng Zhang (chief of Rural Development and Food Security [Agriculture] Thematic Group and concurrently officer-in-charge of Environment Thematic Group), with key contributions from ADB consultants, Victor Tumilba and Lourdes Margarita Caballero.

The manuscript was copyedited by Jess Macasaet (consultant) and proofread by Joy Quitazol-Gonzalez (consultant); page proofs were checked by Layla Amar (consultant); and Rocilyn Locsin Laccay (consultant) took charge of the design and layout.

Publishing guidance was provided by the Knowledge Support Division: Sarah O'Connor (senior communications specialist), Cynthia Hidalgo (senior communications officer, Publishing), Noren Jose (associate communications officer), and April Marie Gallega (associate communications coordinator).

Cecille Villena (consultant), Agnes Patricia A. Magat (senior operations assistant, Environment Thematic Group), Ma. Charina Aguado (associate operations analyst, Environment Thematic Group), Michelle Domingo (senior operations coordination officer), Christopher Darius Tabungar (senior operations assistant, Safeguards Division), and Lucy Ignacio (consultant) gave valuable production and administrative support.

The Environment Thematic Group gratefully acknowledges and extends special thanks to ADB staff and consultants who provided technical inputs and peer reviews: Alexander Nash (urban development specialist), Annabelle C. Giorgetti (senior economist), Arghya Sinha Roy (principal climate change specialist), Belinda Hewitt (disaster risk management specialist), Bruce Dunn (director of Sustainable Development and Climate Change Department Safeguards Division), Charina Cabrido (consultant), Charles Rodgers (consultant), Cristina Velez (consultant), Daniele Ponzi (former chief of the Environment Thematic Group), Geoffrey Wilson (senior water resources specialist), Jingmin Huang (director of Pacific Department Urban Development and Water Division), Junko Sagara (water resources specialist), Karma Yangzom (principal environment specialist), Okju Jeong (consultant), Satoshi Ishii (unit head, project administration), Sonia Chand Sandhu (principal evaluation specialist), Stefan Rau (senior urban development specialist), Suzanne Robertson (principal environment specialist), Thuy Trang Dang (senior urban development specialist), Virinder Sharma (principal urban development specialist), and Yosuke Fukushima (senior climate change specialist). Sincerest appreciation also to Professor Tony Wong of Monash University who provided early insights from his experiences, Kari Davis (technical director of Alliance for Global Water Adaptation–AGWA) for her key contributions in finalizing the manuscript, and Suzanne Ozment (senior associate) from World Resources Institute who served as the external reviewer.

Abbreviations

ADB	Asian Development Bank
CBA	cost–benefit analysis
CCA	climate change adaptation
CEN	country environment note
CPS	country partnership strategy
CRA	climate risk and adaptation assessment
DMC	developing member country
DRM	disaster risk management
EIB	European Investment Bank
EIRR	economic intenal rate of return
HELP	High-Level Experts and Leaders Panel on Water and Disasters
IUCN	International Union for Conservation of Nature
MCA	multicriteria analysis
NAP	national adaptation plan
NBS	nature-based solutions
NDC	Nationally Determined Contribution
NGO	nongovernment organization
PRC	People's Republic of China
TA	technical assistance
UNFCCC	United Nations Framework Convention on Climate Change
USACE	United States Army Corps of Engineers
WWF	World Wildlife Fund

What are Nature-Based Solutions?

In all countries, economic growth comes with the loss of natural capital, our ultimate source of wealth. Therefore, the challenge is combining growth with preserving our ecosystem to secure a more prosperous Asia and the Pacific. Nature-based solutions (NBS) are a potential approach in enhancing the health of our ecosystem. The International Union for Conservation of Nature (IUCN) defines NBS as "actions to protect, sustainably manage, and restore natural or modified ecosystems." These solutions "address societal challenges effectively and adaptively, simultaneously providing human well-being and biodiversity benefits."[1]

NBS also refer to a family of approaches that is designed to formally include ecological processes as services within infrastructure management systems. This means looking at infrastructure challenges with a fresh perspective (Browder et al. 2019) and planning, designing, and financing greener infrastructure in new ways.

Over the past 10 years, climate change, technological innovations, and shifts in development paradigms have increased the need and opportunities to use NBS. This practitioner's guide explains why NBS are important for the Asian Development Bank (ADB) and its stakeholders across the region.

It discusses the benefits of using this approach and how to introduce green options to clients. It will help project officers understand when NBS may be suited to meet longer-term project goals and how to apply these solutions. In addition, this practitioner's guide presents upstream and downstream strategies to develop and carry out NBS projects.

To help readers understand the opportunities and challenges in using NBS, five case studies from Bangladesh, Nepal, the People's Republic of China (PRC), the Philippines, and Viet Nam have been included for reference in the appendixes.[2] These case studies highlight what has worked within ADB to date for successful NBS.

Although NBS are not a panacea, these solutions can still play a crucial role in achieving sustainable and resource-efficient infrastructure. Through this practical guide, the authors aim to help mainstream NBS in ADB and engage a broader group of projects, client staff, and partners to expand the portfolio of available options.

1. Reorienting from Gray to Green: Reasons behind the Growing Interest in Nature-Based Solutions

Many decision-makers, investors, corporations, and donors have shown more interest in greener growth in recent years. There has been a significant demand among investors in mature and developing economies for finance options for green solutions, in general, and NBS. Most financial institutions have also experimented with green investments such as NBS, even if these were one-off or isolated projects. Major engineering and infrastructure organizations have adopted studies that can test the performance of ecosystems relative to hybrid and gray solutions.

---

[1] International Union for Conservation of Nature. Nature-Based Solutions. https://www.iucn.org/theme/nature-based-solutions.

[2] The case studies were developed from interviews with ADB staff and supporting text, largely prepared and written by Ernesto de la Cruz from meetings that he led in person during 2019.

Several factors have fueled the increasing interest in NBS. Three major reasons are discussed in this section: (i) the shift to a broader definition of development that includes social well-being and ecological integrity, (ii) the recognition of the impact of climate change, and (iii) the potential of NBS for disaster risk reduction.

Increased political will to push for sustainable growth

Development has long been viewed as a trade-off between economic growth and natural resources. For at least 2 centuries, we have designed infrastructure that has been very focused on purpose and function. Decision-makers encouraged builders to develop highly optimized projects that were designed to perform reliably for decades.

In the case of water resources management, the standard methodologies that were developed during the 1960s allowed engineers and economists to create effective single-purpose investments. Examples include electrical and wastewater treatment utilities, flood control systems, and irrigation networks (Mendoza et al. 2018). This was largely the pattern of development that originated in North America and Europe through the middle of the 20th century.

However, this approach to development has been widely questioned. The strongest critique has been that economic development is destructive of and/or degrades ecosystems. For instance, most water infrastructure investments in the United States profoundly altered rivers and lakes, causing catastrophic declines in biodiversity and species abundance. These costs were invisible or hidden in the planning and development of these investments. Often, they were simply not considered.

Both North America and Europe saw massive declines in environmental quality together with infrastructure development. In the 1970s and 1980s, moves to better regulate and design these investments to reduce their environmental impacts proved useful. In many cases, it improved water quality in rivers. These regulatory approaches to environmental quality did not fundamentally alter approaches to how we design and plan for infrastructure.

In recent decades, the long-term costs and risks associated with losses to natural systems have been recognized. Growth that causes widespread and lasting damage to ecosystems is not sustainable. They may even reduce critical economic assets in the end. There is a growing consciousness that sophisticated natural solutions can strengthen human and natural ecological relationships and still meet economic goals. Therefore, there is an urgent need for natural sources of capital to be formally recognized as economic assets to ensure deep and lasting economic gains.

These events served as a driving force among decision-makers, civil society, and communities to push for greener projects. There is increasing awareness that green initiatives can help reframe our definition of development. It should reflect a broader vision of resilience that includes not just economic growth but also social well-being and ecological integrity.

Recognition of the impacts of climate change

The second factor behind the growing interest in NBS is climate change. Trends in climate change impacts have created the need for flexible and adaptable solutions. Starting in the 1990s, major global policy initiatives have become aware of the risks of growth that have strayed beyond ecological limits. The Sustainable Development Goals, for instance, focus on well-being while alleviating poverty, conserving natural capital, and building social and human capital (United Nations 2015).

Simultaneously, the United Nations Framework Convention on Climate Change (UNFCCC) has emerged in response to growing and new risks related to a changing climate. This is in recognition that climate change may bring new threats to vulnerable communities, sensitive ecosystems, and long-lived infrastructures and institutions.

Climate change has undermined the case for highly optimized investments. For known or high-confidence climate impacts, it is possible to develop robust approaches to design and planning. But for residual uncertainties that can last for more than 10 years of operations, it is better to choose flexible designs that can evolve and adjust.

NBS are inherently multipurpose investments, and they also lend themselves well to flexible operations and evolving designs (Poff 2018; Matthews et al. 2019; Smith et al. 2019). NBS represent a new generation of approaches that have inherent ecosystem flexibility and adaptability compared to traditional infrastructure solutions. They could be used as solutions given the pressures faced by the ecosystem from shifting climates and insensitive development.

Nature-based solutions as a way to support disaster prevention

Increasing investments in NBS may also increase co-benefits that are not often considered in single-purpose designed infrastructure for disaster risk reduction. According to recent estimates, less than 5% of all funding in the water sector alone goes to NBS (OECD 2020). More recently, many developed countries have begun to question old assumptions. The Netherlands Delta Commission, for instance, suggested in a 2008 report that natural systems can reliably perform many critical infrastructure functions, and these systems may provide co-benefits that offer more significant returns on investment than traditional approaches (Deltacommissie 2008).

Over the past decade, the Netherlands has become a global leader in NBS, in particular, since government and civil society now see NBS as specially qualified to support disaster prevention efforts, particularly for flood risk (Anderson et al. 2019). A partnership of Asian and European governments led by Japan and the Netherlands has also begun to question an overreliance on a defensive approach to disaster risk management (DRM), shifting many new projects to a prevention approach to reduce risks before extreme events occur rather than focusing on DRM as a "reaction" through recovery and rebuilding efforts. When rebuilding does occur following a disaster, there is also a greater emphasis on "building back better," so that prevention is included within recovery programs (HELP Water & Disasters 2019).

Other countries such as the United Kingdom show similar patterns. Efforts to lower disaster risk for population centers such as London have moved upstream into rural areas, where working with farmers and other resource managers can make modest, cost-effective changes in landscape management that can have large reductions in downstream flood risk. These efforts are supported in many cases by commercial insurance entities, who see a significant return on their investment in NBS (OECD 2019).

Examples of public and private sector nature-based solutions initiatives

Several key finance and government institutions have recently signaled a major shift in priorities to promote, advocate, and support the systematic implementation of NBS solutions. In 2017, for instance, the European Investment Bank (EIB) launched an NBS loan financing program called the Natural Capital Finance Facility, initially capitalized at some €25 million (EIB 2019).

More recently, the Green Climate Fund has launched a set of NBS project guidelines, especially for climate adaptation. In addition, World Bank (2019a) released a report on integrating green and gray infrastructure solutions for operational investments in transportation and water (Browder et al. 2019). This builds on earlier work that looked in more detail at specific regional and thematic priorities. These priorities include disaster risk reduction programs in the Asia and Pacific region (Li, Turner, and Jiang 2012) and NBS, more generally, for water and ecosystem priorities (Quesne et al. 2010).

The Inter-American Development Bank has also recently started mainstreaming NBS (Silva et al. 2020) and several large-scale NBS projects, such as a national-scale climate-resilient environmental flows policy program with a national water agency. Many aid agencies have been rolling out NBS projects, such as the Foreign,

Commonwealth & Development Office;[3] Deutsche Gesellschaft für Internationale Zusammenarbeit GmbH (GIZ); United States Agency for International Development; Swiss Agency for Cooperation and Development; and the Swedish International Development Cooperation Agency. FMO, the Dutch entrepreneurial development bank, and SNV Netherlands Development Organisation launched a joint NBS partnership development program with World Wildlife Fund (WWF) in 2019 (WWF 2019).

A few governments have also been exploring large-scale NBS implementation programs. Beginning in 2009, the Netherlands began an ambitious NBS and traditional infrastructure program focusing on climate adaptation, especially that associated with riparian and coastal flood risks, including coastal erosion. In 2019, the Dutch Treasury Ministry issued a €5 billion green bond to finance a relatively new NBS approach called "room for the river," which supports controlled flooding of multipurpose floodplains, particularly those designated as riparian ecosystems and riparian protected areas (Smith et al. 2019). Following Superstorm Sandy (also called Hurricane Sandy) in North America, the United States Army Corps of Engineers (USACE) launched a large-scale coastal erosion reduction program that included both NBS and hybrid approaches that have been used extensively on the United States Atlantic coast (Bridges 2015).

The "sponge city" movement in the PRC has been a significant influence in East Asia (e.g., Appendix 1). Somewhat like room for the river, sponge cities have designated flood zones, often using NBS to slow runoff, increase absorption, limit physical damage, and improve water quality. In most cases, the NBS have provisions for recreation, water quality, and ecological services as well. Conceptually, sponge cities place urban areas in the context of a larger ecological and hydrological landscape that normalizes flooding as a natural process.

Private sector and private investor NBS applications are increasing globally as well. The Climate Bonds Initiative has been releasing sector criteria for climate-resilient NBS in areas such as water, transport, forests, agriculture, and land use change. These criteria are intended to communicate to investors that a particular project is credible in terms of its ecological and resilience benefits—that the bond issuer is not "greenwashing" a weak or even environmentally negative project (CBI 2018). Several urban utilities, for instance, have applied the criteria for NBS projects in regions as diverse as Cape Town, South Africa; San Francisco, United States; and Beijing, PRC.

Civil society, intergovernmental institutions, and environmental nongovernment organizations (NGOs) have also continued to expand their work around NBS in recent years. ADB has published the Guidelines for Mainstreaming Natural River Management in Water Sector Investments (ADB 2021). The WWF released a "green guide" for NBS approaches to flooding (WWF 2017). The Nature Conservancy has promoted source water protection, in general, and many regional and basin-scale water funds on a global basis to ensure that the ecological aspects of water resources are funded and institutionalized (Abell et al. 2017). The IUCN has worked in the Lower Mekong Region on a variety of NBS projects intended to promote water security more generally (IUCN 2020). These approaches are significantly more sophisticated than NBS projects from previous decades. The timeline of how NBS as a concept has evolved is also illustrated in the 2016 publication of the IUCN.

---

[3]   The Foreign, Commonwealth & Development Office of the United Kingdom was created on 2 September 2020 through the merger of the Foreign & Commonwealth Office (FCO) and the Department for International Development (DFID).

2.   Definitions of Nature-Based Solutions

NBS is a relatively new term (Nesshöver et al. 2017; WWAP and UN Water 2018). The European Union has defined NBS as "actions which are inspired by, supported by, or copied from nature" (Bauduceau et al. 2015).

The IUCN definition of NBS as "actions to protect, sustainably manage, and restore natural or modified ecosystems" has become standard in many institutions, including the United Nations Environment Programme. A critical aspect of the IUCN definition is the human-centered purpose of the NBS, which aligns with how *any* type of infrastructure has been traditionally defined. The IUCN definition is especially important for why NBS is used. Even if co-benefits to ecosystems are critical to a particular NBS, the asset is ultimately meant to support our communities and economies. For this guide, the IUCN definition of NBS will be used.

Older terms also capture the different nuances of NBS. These include ecosystem services, environmental reserves, ecological engineering (or sometimes eco-engineering), biomimicry, green infrastructure, and hybrid infrastructure. Some related terms may reflect specific applications of NBS, such as ecosystem-based adaptation, natural and nature-based features, and green adaptation.

NBS are designed to formally include ecological processes as services within infrastructure management systems. In some cases, these approaches may include creating an explicit management process that recognizes functions and services that are already provided by a specific ecosystem. An example is existing wetlands that can remove sediment and nutrient runoff from a set of farmers' fields. These wetlands should be protected and actively monitored and managed so that services can be maintained or enhanced. Such NBS are sometimes referred to as "natural features" (Bridges 2015).

NBS can also refer to highly engineered systems that make active use of natural processes. These NBS are often quite technical in their development and management. An example is the use of managed aquifer recharge as a groundwater reservoir for water treatment and/or storage (Dillon et al. 2010). There is also the use of coastal geomorphological processes for the so-called "sand motor" (also called sand engine) off the coastline of the Netherlands. It replenishes coastal areas experiencing active erosion, but it was actively built (Brière et al. 2018).

Even so, other definitions can provide some sense of how the practice of NBS continues to evolve. Following damage from several large and damaging tropical cyclones in the first 15 years of this century, the USACE began testing the explicit use of NBS in a wide variety of settings, which they distinguished into two categories:

> Natural features are created through the action of physical, geological, biological, and chemical processes over time. Nature-based features, in contrast, are created by human design, engineering, and construction (in concert with natural processes) to provide specific services such as coastal risk reduction and other ecosystem services (e.g., habitat for fish and wildlife). Nature-based features are acted upon by processes operating in nature, and as a result, generally must be maintained by human intervention in order to sustain the functions and services for which they were built (Bridges 2015).

The USACE definition distinguishes between natural features—existing ecological assets (such as an aquifer or river) even if they have been modified or enhanced in some way—and nature-based features, which are fully designed and engineered assets that use natural materials and processes as core to operations.

The nature-based features are essentially a built form of green infrastructure that may mimic ecological processes or systems. These distinctions may be important for resource managers, environmental regulators, and the engineering professionals involved in their planning, operation, and maintenance. The USACE definition is especially important for those engaged in the technical process of developing, designing, and applying engineered NBS projects.

3. Critiques of Nature-Based Solutions

NBS have been increasing in their adoption and deployment. Even so, different audiences have continued to criticize NBS for the following reasons:

1. **Nature-based solutions lack evidence for efficacy.**

    Perhaps the oldest and most widespread criticism of NBS is that, for many years, there were only a few available successful NBS cases. Today, there are many examples and several projects run into millions or even billions of dollars. For the most part, these examples come from very developed countries. This is often an obstacle because it makes these projects seem removed or less relevant from the experience and awareness of policymakers and technical partners of ADB clients. Moreover, the function of some ecosystems may be different between two countries, for example, Germany and Mongolia.

    Often, local evidence for a specific NBS approach is a more important obstacle today than more general concerns about proof of concept. However, these issues can often be addressed through pilot projects and/or more local knowledge. The number of systematic studies that look at evidence does, in some cases, remain small (e.g., International Hydropower Association 2019; OECD 2020; Cooper and Matthews 2020). However, strong evidence is available for almost all types of NBS.

2. **Nature-based solution projects are a luxury the developing world cannot afford, as they slow down or redirect investment.**

    Many fast-growing countries within Asia have largely followed the same development strategies used in western countries, such as in Japan, the Republic of Korea, Singapore, and the PRC. Countries just starting to accelerate their infrastructure investments may see little reason to modify this development model: what worked in the PRC should also work in Viet Nam. NBS represent, however, a powerful model for how development can accelerate. This is much like how telecoms in Asia largely skipped the use of transmission wires in place of wireless mobile networks. They provide better service over a broader area at cheaper costs. NBS represent a leap forward in planning and design for more lasting economic development, not a reversal.

3. **Nature-based solution projects come from advocacy, not real comparisons with gray solutions.**

    In practice, many of the loudest voices for NBS come from environmental NGOs and civil society. Some of these communications may not provide convincing arguments for decision-makers considering NBS solutions. This guide and other resources cited here highlight that the economic and development cases for considering NBS are strong.

4. **Proponents lack experience in designing and deploying nature-based solutions.**

    This is a genuine concern in many agencies, partners, and countries, including within ADB itself. However, investment in early NBS projects can include capacity building elements that can create a virtuous circle that, with success, can lead to more and more mainstreamed consideration of NBS for the future.

5. **There is a need to make exceptions in traditional planning, design, evaluation, maintenance, and finance processes.**

    Again, there is a concern of a mismatch between the needs for developing NBS projects and traditional gray infrastructure, which is valid and important to recognize. Procurement systems for a traditional wastewater treatment facility will be completely different than for a wetland capable of treating the same quantity of effluent to the same quality. This guide is designed to help with these constraints within ADB's systems. These obstacles should also become lower and less important over time and with more projects.

II Benefits of Nature-Based Solutions for Managing Climate and Disaster Risks

This chapter looks at two areas: (i) designing for resilience using nature-based solutions (NBS), and (ii) the high-level benefits that NBS can provide relative to more traditional types of assets and investments.

1. Designing for Resilience Using Nature-Based Solutions

The Intergovernmental Panel on Climate Change defines resilience as "the ability of a system and its component parts to anticipate, absorb, accommodate, or recover from the effects of a hazardous event in a timely and efficient manner, including through ensuring the preservation, restoration, or improvement of its essential basic structures and functions" (Intergovernmental Panel on Climate Change 2012). Other definitions exist for climate resilience, but the panel's definition captures some of the core concepts associated with both climate change adaptation (CCA) and disaster risk management (DRM).

Some definitions of resilience are broader and cover emerging topics, such as pandemic resilience. Even though they share many of the same core concepts as climate resilience (ADB 2020), NBS are widely viewed as a new tool and asset class for addressing climate and disaster risks and as an instrument for building resilience (Matthews et al. 2019). However, this framing begs the question: what is resilience, and can NBS be as or more effective in contributing to resilience in practice?

ADB's Urban Climate Change Resilience Trust Fund lists seven qualities of resilient systems described by the engineering firm Arup for their City Resilience Framework: reflective, robust, redundant, flexible, resourceful, inclusive, and integrated (2014). Table 1 suggests how NBS interact with and support these seven qualities.

Table 1: Resilient System Qualities and Contributions of Nature-Based Solutions

Resilient System Quality	Definition	Nature-Based Solution Contribution to Resilience
Reflective	• Reflective systems accept increasing uncertainty and change. They have mechanisms to continuously evolve and will modify standards or norms based on emerging evidence, rather than seeking permanent solutions based on the status quo. • As a result, people and institutions examine and systematically learn from their past experiences and leverage this learning to inform future decision-making.	• Nature-based solutions (NBS) are normally self-correcting and evolving systems. They adjust to shifts in their ambient conditions and often with self-stabilizing and self-repairing qualities. • They are also historical systems so their past and present will influence their future evolution.
Robust	• Robust systems include well-thought-of, built, and managed physical assets so they can withstand the impacts of hazardous events without huge damage or loss of function. • Robust design anticipates potential failures in systems. It makes provision so failure is predictable, safe, and not disproportionate to the cause. It avoids overreliance on a single asset, cascading failure, and design thresholds that might lead to catastrophic collapse, if exceeded.	• Through green–gray hybrid approaches, NBS can be used to support and reinforce more traditional infrastructure and increase overall system robustness. • The hybrid approach allows the distribution of risk across a wider set of assets. This can reduce the risk of critical failure of a single piece of infrastructure.

continued on next page

Table 1 continued

Resilient System Quality	Definition	Nature-Based Solution Contribution to Resilience
Redundant	• Redundancy refers to spare capacity purposely created within systems to make room for disruption, extreme pressures, or surges in demand. It includes diversity or the multiple ways to achieve a given need or fulfill a function. Examples include distributed infrastructure networks and resource reserves. • Redundancies should be intentional, cost-effective, and prioritized at a citywide scale. It should not be an externality of inefficient design.	• Green–gray approaches can create system redundancy when both traditional and NBS are used to support system function. Using both approaches reduces the reliance of a single piece of infrastructure. It also minimizes the risk of critical system failure. • The inherent growth of living NBS (e.g., coastal forests) creates a dynamic redundancy.
Flexible	• Flexibility implies that systems can change, evolve, and adapt in response to changing circumstances. This may favor decentralized and modular approaches to infrastructure or ecosystem management. • Flexibility can be achieved through the introduction of new knowledge and technologies, as needed. • It also means considering and using indigenous or traditional knowledge and practices in new ways.	• NBS are inherently flexible solutions. They evolve with the changing environment and adapt to system externalities. They are typically much easier to undo and adjust than hard and gray infrastructure. They can also be eliminated, or the management radically altered, if conditions and needs shift over time. • NBS allow the incorporation of indigenous and traditional knowledge into modern technical practices.
Resourceful	• Resourcefulness implies that people and institutions can rapidly find different ways to achieve their goals or meet their needs during a shock or when under stress. This may include investing in capacity to anticipate future conditions, set priorities, and respond, for example, by mobilizing and coordinating wider human, financial, and physical resources. • Resourcefulness is instrumental to a city's ability to restore functionality of critical systems, potentially under severely constrained conditions.	• In the case of traditional infrastructure failure, NBS can provide resources that can be used during times of stress. • NBS can also be used as a stopgap solution while repairs to traditional infrastructure are made. Because the history of natural systems is often essential to their function, they can often respond to rare or extreme events quite effectively and reliably.
Inclusive	• Inclusion emphasizes the need for broad consultation and engagement of communities, including the most vulnerable groups. • Addressing the shocks or stresses faced by one sector, location, or community in isolation of others is an anathema to the notion of resilience. An inclusive approach contributes to a sense of shared ownership or a joint vision to build city resilience.	• As opposed to large-scale gray infrastructure, NBS can be smaller and less expensive. This makes them more integrated into community management practices and increases a sense of ownership. • NBS can also yield environmental and social benefits that support community improvement. In rural areas and in places with significant foraging, NBS are often deeply integrated with human livelihoods. In some cases, NBS also provide spiritual and ritual functions and services.
Integrated	• Integration and alignment between city systems promotes consistency in decision-making and ensures that all investments are mutually supportive to a common outcome. • Integration is evident within and between resilient systems, and across different scales of their operation. Exchange of information between systems enables them to function collectively and respond rapidly through shorter feedback loops throughout the city.	• NBS are inherently integrated approaches. They connect new and existing systems across all operational scales. • NBS can communicate without human intervention or aid, though they often reach their highest levels of efficacy by active management and decision-making within human systems.

Source: Adapted from Arup. 2014. *City Resilience Framework*. City Resilience Index. New York: The Rockefeller Foundation.
https://www.arup.com/perspectives/publications/research/section/city-resilience-index.

Another perspective on NBS and resilience comes from ADB's holistic approach in delivering the Strategy 2030 priority of building disaster and climate resilience. ADB envisions the four dimensions of resilience as ecological, physical, social and institutional, and financial resilience (Figure 1). NBS can aid ADB to bolster resilience activities in all four dimensions.

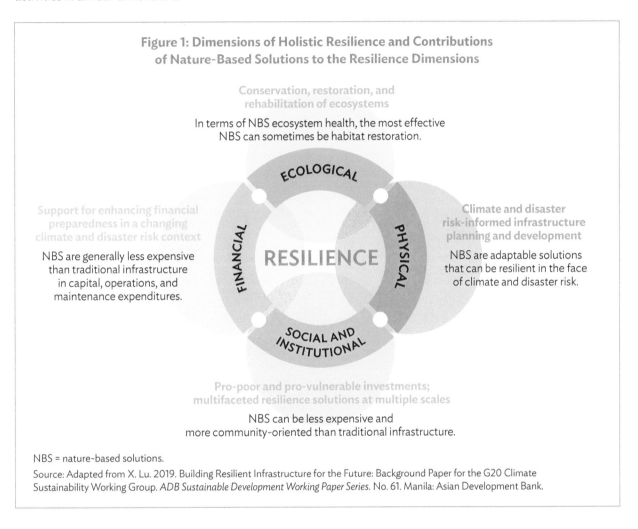

Figure 1: Dimensions of Holistic Resilience and Contributions of Nature-Based Solutions to the Resilience Dimensions

Conservation, restoration, and rehabilitation of ecosystems

In terms of NBS ecosystem health, the most effective NBS can sometimes be habitat restoration.

ECOLOGICAL

Support for enhancing financial preparedness in a changing climate and disaster risk context

NBS are generally less expensive than traditional infrastructure in capital, operations, and maintenance expenditures.

FINANCIAL

RESILIENCE

PHYSICAL

Climate and disaster risk-informed infrastructure planning and development

NBS are adaptable solutions that can be resilient in the face of climate and disaster risk.

SOCIAL AND INSTITUTIONAL

Pro-poor and pro-vulnerable investments; multifaceted resilience solutions at multiple scales

NBS can be less expensive and more community-oriented than traditional infrastructure.

NBS = nature-based solutions.
Source: Adapted from X. Lu. 2019. Building Resilient Infrastructure for the Future: Background Paper for the G20 Climate Sustainability Working Group. *ADB Sustainable Development Working Paper Series*. No. 61. Manila: Asian Development Bank.

Historically, economic investments have strongly favored hard, gray infrastructure that focused on a single or small range of purposes. With time, most governments and multilateral development banks have recognized that a broader set of solutions needs to be considered and implemented in a variety of sectors. Gray solutions will continue to be critical throughout Asia and the Pacific.

ADB staff and clients, however, have found that both green and hybrid NBS projects can meet or exceed cost–performance criteria of comparable gray investments while also supporting other agenda. This includes quality of life, ecological resilience, and flexibility in the face of climate and economic uncertainty.

ADB's vision for the 21st century recognizes both traditional and emerging challenges, including disaster risk management and climate change impacts. These two areas of investment represent significant opportunities for an expanded set of solutions, beyond the traditional portfolio of gray solutions. Climate change has revealed how rigid, inflexible approaches to infrastructure may have inherent weaknesses as climate impacts continue to accrue and expand (Matthews et al. 2019). In contrast, NBS approaches have inherent advantages to manage uncertainties in disaster and climate risk.

In many cases, ADB staff have already been implementing NBS. Many ADB clients have also been exploring NBS options within specific sectors. Examples are presented in Table 2.

Table 2: Examples of Nature-Based Solutions Projects in ADB Developing Member Countries

Sector	Project	Purpose
Cities	Sponge cities in the People's Republic of China (Appendix 1)	To reduce urban flood risk by linking rural land use patterns with water management and by creating urban wetlands to absorb floodwaters
Water	Flood risk reduction in the Philippines (Appendix 2)	To develop a "room for the river" approach to reduce flood risks for both local and downstream assets and communities
Transport	Wildlife corridors in Nepal and Bangladesh (Appendix 3)	To improve regional road networks while retaining and improving habitat connectivity throughout a major protected area

Source: Asian Development Bank. 2020. *Protecting and Investing in Natural Capital in Asia and the Pacific: A Practitioner's Guide to Nature-Based Solutions*. Consultant's report. Manila (TA 9461-REG). https://www.adb.org/sites/default/files/project-documents/50159/50159-001-tacr-en_3.pdf.

2.   Benefits of High-Level Nature-Based Solutions Relative to More Traditional Types of Assets and Investments

These advantages and benefits are often important for ADB staff. Many clients, especially those unfamiliar with NBS approaches, may need to have a more explicit set of advantages and disadvantages to consider. The focus here will be on two bodies of work within ADB: CCA and DRM. CCA and DRM are of course connected. Many climate impacts are associated with severe disasters, while climate change is altering the frequency, intensity, and extent of many disasters. NBS open the range of approaches that can be provided to ADB clients and partners in both areas.

1.   The **multipurpose focus of NBS** has been widely discussed for decades, usually as co-benefits that NBS provide beyond the primary or nominal purpose, such as **drought defense or water treatment** (WWAP and UN Water 2018). Co-benefits represent the additional advantages that come from a project beyond its primary (or perhaps primary and secondary) goal.

For instance, the use of a riparian wetland for flood mitigation may also support local fisheries, household building supplies, water quality, recreation, erosion control, biodiversity, and water nutrient management. Formally accounting for these co-benefits within a traditional single-purpose cost–benefit framework has proven to be challenging in many cases; multicriteria analysis has become a widespread alternative approach for analyzing co-benefits (e.g., Silva et al. 2020). At the same time, these co-benefits may be the most critical element in promoting adoption with policymakers and stakeholders as well as co-investors (e.g., Appendix 5). Generally, traditional gray infrastructure investments do not track co-benefits.

However, co-benefits can be transformative and fundamental to the conception of a project. For instance, in Udon Thani, Thailand, a variety of gray, hybrid, and NBS approaches were considered for both urban stormwater retention and water storage for dry periods. Stakeholders with vested interests included energy producers, paddy irrigators, and residents and businesses with assets exposed to increasing flood risks.

While traditional solutions were considered to handle each of these needs separately, local authorities chose to merge the issues into a single "problem shed" that could be solved by building a series of lakes within the city. These urban lakes would be capable of performing the core functions provided by gray infrastructure at an acceptable performance level while also improving the quality of life within the city, overall promoting an integration of ecological, sector, and community concerns (Smith et al. 2019).

2. More recently, groups such as the Organisation for Economic Co-operation and Development and the World Bank have argued for a new set of advantages relating to NBS, including the **ability to complement traditional infrastructure approaches; the ability to mitigate biodiversity loss**; and perhaps most recently, **the ability to reduce climate change risks** (OECD 2020).

3. While specific projects may vary, many promoters of NBS also like to point out that green projects have less obvious benefits, such as **greater ease in reversing or altering the use of the investment, broader public satisfaction**, and, in many cases, **lower construction and installation costs** (Smith et al. 2019).

Across Asia and the Pacific, NBS have become increasingly important and recognized as a viable set of solutions. The private sector has even begun to refocus on NBS in places like Indonesia and the Philippines (Box 1). Economies such as Singapore and Hong Kong, China, for instance, have recognized that the development choices made by the United States and Western Europe in the 20th century are being reversed and reworked. They have realized that they do not need to recapitulate these lessons.

By making greener investments now, Asia can avoid the environmental degradation and lower quality of life that traditional western approaches to infrastructure planning, design, and operations have promoted. For many Pacific islands, large single-purpose investments never made economic or cultural sense. More decentralized green and hybrid investments can help reinforce traditional livelihoods while also showing progress against national and global economic development standards (World Bank 2019a).

Box 1: Private Sector Investment in Nature-Based Solutions: Indonesia and the Philippines

In the city of Semarang, Indonesia, a mix of green and gray infrastructure approaches were proposed to combat urban flooding, land subsidence, and landslide risk caused by population growth and urban expansion, extreme rainfall events, and sea level rise. An investment program utilizing five clusters—micro-interventions, spongy mountain, rechanneling the city, feeding the industry, and recharging the aquifer—was proposed to increase water storage and infiltration, increase surface water availability and consumption (as compared to groundwater consumption), and significantly decrease groundwater extraction. For example, the spongy mountain cluster involves the reforestation of mountain terraces to allow for reduced landslide and flood risk and better water supply. This approach recognizes the role of ecosystems as critical infrastructure and a key component of systemic resilience.

The goal of the program is to reinforce the connection between economic growth (Sustainable Development Goal 8) and the achievements of water security (Sustainable Development Goal 6) in the climate change context. Political and financial instruments are considered along with green and gray infrastructure to meet these goals and make the city more resilient. The project is designed to be first implemented through a few pioneer transactions and then scaled up to the whole city to limit stakeholder's resistance to change and allow for sufficient implementation capacity from the public and private sectors. Therefore, an enabling environment could be created for public and private sector collaboration, alongside multilateral development banks. Implementation of approximately one project per cluster will begin in 2020.

Blended finance can also be utilized to make untraditional and potentially risky projects, such as green or green–gray infrastructure, more desirable to investors. Blended finance is the combination of public and philanthropic capital, such as that from a multilateral development bank, to increase private sector investment. Proposing this type of funding mechanism can be used as a tool to promote investment in nature-based solutions.

continued on next page

Box 1 *continued*

For example, in 2008 the Government of the Philippines, the United States Agency for International Development, and the Japan Bank for International Cooperation established the Philippine Water Revolving Fund (PWRF) to combine public and private financing to lower borrowing rates and to market projects to additional private finance institutions. This financial mechanism resulted in the mobilization of additional domestic commercial funds for water utility, and water, sanitation, and hygiene projects. Between 2008 and 2014, more than $234 million in loans were channeled through the PWRF for these projects, of which approximately 60% of the funding came from private banks.

The PWRF's success in building confidence in the blended finance approach also influenced domestic banks to start supporting water projects on their own, which was previously not something typically done. One of the lessons learned from this project was that blending through the revolving fund has resulted in lower borrowing costs for water service providers and longer tenors. Second, the different credit enhancements offered with the PWRF lowered investment risk. Finally, the multilayered approach of the PWRF to mobilize commercial finance is important to bear in mind.

Sources: M. Altamirano. 2019. *Hybrid (Green–Gray) Water Security Strategies: A Blended Finance Approach for Implementation at Scale.* Background paper for the Roundtable on Financing Water Regional Meeting. Manila. 26–27 November. https://www.oecd.org/water/Session3b.Hybrid_(green-gray)_water_security_strategies.pdf; MLA+ et al. 2019. *Semarang Cascading Semarang: Steps to Inclusive Growth (Phase II Report).* https://drive.google.com/file/d/1J9lxNCfe0txR8rvUkrvFprCKkdqnICTt/preview.

III Initiating Green Options with Clients

Nature-based solutions (NBS) have many advantages. But as with any other category of investment, they can be designed or implemented (or maintained) poorly, and they may not be appropriate for all types of uses or all clients. Early discussions with ADB partners and clients should be a joint exploration to determine when, where, and how a range of solutions—including green and hybrid approaches—may be relevant.

However, achieving greener solutions will not always be straightforward, especially at first. In some cases, clients may suggest NBS as a useful investment option on their own. We should see clients bring up NBS options themselves more frequently over time, especially as more ADB NBS options successfully reach fruition.

In any case, successful implementation of NBS often comes at the end of a long chain of events. While technical design and economic issues are extremely important considerations, ADB staff who have managed or implemented NBS projects all emphasize the importance of ensuring that NBS options are discussed early with clients and partners. These early discussions can make the retention and development of effective NBS much easier—or much harder.

1. Eight Questions to Consider When Looking at Nature-Based Solutions

Ideally, this practitioner's guide should help ensure that better NBS options are considered viable projects on par with traditional infrastructure and natural resources interventions. However, NBS should not be viewed dogmatically. They are not appropriate for all projects or similar projects in different contexts.

Good NBS will contain high value and relevance to ADB and client objectives; although, many traditional gray investments can be made more ecologically sustainable. Hard and fast rules on these issues do not exist, but some "pre"-prefeasibility considerations for looking at NBS include the following issues:

(i)   Does the client or client agency raise objections that seem very difficult to overcome, such as a recent catastrophic failure of an NBS project that makes these options politically unacceptable?

(ii)   Can capacity gaps be identified in advance? Will technical assistance (TA) and support be available for early project development steps with domestic consultants or partners? If not, are there sufficient resources for international consultants or partners to participate?

(iii) How time-sensitive is the project? For clients and ADB project officers still new to NBS options, green projects may require more time or resources than a comparable gray investment.

(iv)   Can you find successful local, national, or regional analogs for the type of NBS investment you are considering? If so, these may bode well moving forward, since the project may be more tangible and clearer to develop. Green approaches to coastal erosion, for instance, are relatively widespread, while managed aquifer recharge is much less common.

- Can you find established practices or guidelines for the type of project you are considering? For instance, a broad literature exists for the use of wetlands for wastewater treatment, at least at small scales.

- Is an NBS approach to your project considered experimental in the Asia and Pacific region? Globally?

(v) What will happen to your project if performance objectives are not met? Will the overall project fail? Are there options for increasing redundancy? Are there options for piloting as well as for scaling if an experiment proves successful?

(vi) Regions with recent conflict or very weak governance are probably poor candidates for projects that may require extensive maintenance and long-standing capacity. For instance, for climate adaptation projects, flexibility may be an inappropriate climate strategy since such an approach assumes strong institutions capable of learning and retaining lessons over decades. Simpler, more robust projects may be most appropriate in such circumstances.

(vii) Are you considering green components of a larger gray project or a completely green project? For instance, ADB's South Asia Subregional Economic Cooperation Roads Improvement Program in Nepal and Bangladesh was largely an adjustment of an otherwise straightforward transport project that aimed to reduce the impact on local wildlife populations (Appendix 3). Likewise, the "Green Cities" project in Viet Nam was extensively modified based on its NBS design relative to a more traditional project with a similar purpose, but the overall scale of the project was relatively small (Appendix 4). A large sponge cities approach can have many complex elements and may not be a good initial endeavor for a project officer.

(viii) Can you identify allies within ADB and/or partner institutions who can support you with key aspects? Examples include the following:

- Prefeasibility,
- Finding effective technical support,
- Cost–benefit analysis or multicriteria analysis,
- Capacity building with clients,
- Procurement, and
- Ensuring effective handoff to clients.

If your answers to many of these questions are negative or "not right now," you may want to defer the project, reduce expectations with your client, increase the time frame for implementation, or alter the scale and scope of the project. Alternatively, you might want to consider how to reframe the range of solutions from gray to green with your client.

2. Checklist for Testing Nature-Based Solutions Readiness and Suitability for ADB Partners

ADB staff should be aware that including hybrid or green solutions will almost certainly add to the complexity of the client's work. This is true in many countries and institutions with limited NBS experience. Even under the best of circumstances and even when green assets have clear advantages and opportunities relative to gray assets, there will be challenges in introducing NBS.

Although there may be no obstacles to acceptance, there may be issues around developing a design, finding institutional support or consultants, arranging financing, assessing costs and benefits, and determining responsibilities between implementing and regulatory agencies. These may slow otherwise clear processes as the client approaches these issues for the first few green projects.

Proponents should then expect that these early projects would take somewhat longer and/or trace a different trajectory than a traditional project development cycle may otherwise follow. Institutional obstacles can be overcome, but the potential for caution and concern by clients should be appreciated and anticipated.

Some clients may also have stronger concerns about NBS. Institutional burdens may seem excessive or impossible. In countries with very limited experience with NBS, green solutions may be viewed as either "inferior" investments that will deliver lower quality benefits or a "luxury approach" that is inappropriate for a developing country context.

NBS solutions are as diverse as traditional gray investments in their shape, performance, and range of potential outcomes. However, if the partnering institution has limited experience with NBS, a few bad cases can poison and bias technical and senior staff against reattempting NBS—even if you are proposing a fundamentally different type of project. Below is a checklist of questions to help test the NBS readiness and suitability for ADB partners.

(i) Has your agency or department attempted to design and build green and/or hybrid projects to date? If yes:

- Was it for this category of investment or infrastructure or for a different sector or type of infrastructure?
- Was the project completed? If not, why not?
- How was the project initiated?

  – Was technical analysis challenging?
  – How was the project financed?

- Why was a green approach selected?
- What challenges arose with the project?
- How did decision-makers and stakeholders respond to the proposal?
- Was there sufficient capacity internally to complete the project? Were outside groups or consultants used to complete critical components?
- Did the project meet or exceed performance expectations? If not, why not?
- Would your agency be willing to pursue additional NBS projects in the future? If not, why not?

(ii) How are NBS perceived by the following stakeholders: agency leadership, key stakeholders, politicians, local businesses, voters?

(iii) Can projects that potentially span several ministries or other key stakeholders be coordinated to develop more holistic solutions, such as energy, agriculture, urban resilience, and disaster risk management (DRM)?

(iv) Have you or your leadership seen successful NBS projects in peer organizations, such as in neighboring countries or interacting agencies or other institutions within your country?

(v) Have you been interested in exploring NBS approaches like those developed by global thought leaders, such as in Singapore, Australia, or Europe?

(vi) Is there an existing regulatory framework for NBS or design guidance specifications by professional organizations such as utility groups or engineering societies?

(vii) Is there national-scale expertise available in your agency, among local consultants or firms, or in local universities to support the planning and design of NBS?

(viii) Are conditions favorable for co-funding or co-development of NBS with local and national institutions, such as through green bonds, city and national cooperation, and coordination with relevant industry and business groups?

3. How to Reframe Discussions from "Gray versus Green" to "Gray and Green"

Very few specific client needs can be met exclusively through NBS. However, many transport, urban, and water management needs can be met along a gray–green spectrum of solutions, from traditional gray infrastructure investments to, in some cases, fully ecosystem-based assets and approaches. Moreover, NBS can be especially effective in situations where climate adaptation and DRM interventions are necessary.

In all cases, if ADB staff believe that NBS may be relevant, even if just as a component or option, then the topic of nontraditional approaches should be introduced as early as possible with clients and partners. Ideally, this process should allow ADB and client staff to make direct comparisons and tradeoffs in terms of efficacy, resilience, costs, co-benefits, and other significant qualities.

1. **Talk about developing member country and ADB partner needs at the correct scale.**

    Often, ADB partners will describe issues and concerns that a project is intended to address at very local scales—perhaps even just the intended site for development. By elevating the physical size of the area being discussed, such as upstream and downstream localities, NBS can emerge in a powerful and quite "natural" way, as a mechanism to discuss how landscapes are interacting with the intended outcomes of the work.

    If landscapes and ecosystems are not supporting the project, even if they are quite far from the site, then ecological restoration, enhancement, and protection may be early vehicles for bringing NBS into the range of acceptable approaches to consider. Similarly, the intended timescale of discussion can be important as an entry point. Ecosystems may have played critical roles in the issue at hand in the past, and their role may be expected to evolve and shift with climate and economic changes. In either case, NBS can operate over longer timescales than most forms of built infrastructure and they can serve to ensure the effective longevity and reliability of built and hybrid assets if they are integrated into planning and operations.

2. **Introduce nature-based solutions early in the dialogue.**

    Discussing NBS after technical and financial discussions have already been initiated with traditional gray solutions is often much more difficult to explore. Depending on the attitudes and familiarity of partner institutions, expectations for the shape of the project and range of potential solutions may be much more limited.

    ADB staff, who have implemented NBS throughout the region, regularly encounter a diversity of definitions of "green" (e.g., Appendix 3). As suggested in Chapter 1, NBS exist along a spectrum, from explicitly including an existing and intact ecological landscape into a management regime to a highly engineered bioremediation wetland designed for treating heavy metals suspended in surface flows. Many—and perhaps most—ADB clients are already experimenting with greener approaches, some of which may reflect more regional or national criteria for "green." As ADB staff, you should be able to draw upon a global data set of examples and criteria. Do not be afraid to make a "light green" project "bright green"—or at least a brighter shade of green (e.g., Appendix 2).

3. **Discuss a variety of potential solutions and prepare to answer concerns about nature-based solutions.**

    Clients will vary significantly in their level of familiarity, readiness, and level of comfort on NBS, both as individuals and as partner institutions. Discussing the relative advantages and disadvantages of a wide range of potential solutions shows clients you respect their needs and concerns and can ensure that NBS become and remain a viable option. Major points of discussion include the following:

(i) Are NBS a suitable option as a potential strategy?

A justifiable concern for many clients and partners is the suitability of green and hybrid solutions, especially early in the country strategy process and during strategic engagement and project development processes. It is important for ADB staff to acknowledge with skeptical partners that NBS are not suitable for all projects and contexts. While mangrove forests reduce coastal flooding and erosion in many circumstances, they may not provide sufficient protection for low-lying coastal communities or critical economic assets against large storm surges.

Wetlands cannot generate hydropower. Yet, wetlands and mangroves can help support gray infrastructure designs and operations, and potentially alter how they interact with the larger landscape. While freshwater ecosystems can provide remarkable water filtration benefits, not all utilities can operate a piece of green infrastructure without significant adjustments in policies, staff, and financing, such as in countries with a recent history of civil unrest or conflict. Flexible approaches to climate resilience and infrastructure operation may require institutional capacities that are too challenging to build for now.

(ii) Do ADB partners acknowledge flaws with traditional solutions?

At the same time, most technical and high-level decision-makers have long assumed that the most progressive and advanced approaches to infrastructure eliminated natural features. Hence, highly engineered, often quite technical installations of stone, steel, and concrete were created. It's now known that expensive, high-profile projects are not guaranteed to perform well, especially in a shifting climate. Furthermore, because losses to ecosystems, livelihoods, or in quality of life have not been tracked or calculated, that does not mean these losses do not exist.

Defining problems in very narrow ways—e.g., moving stormwater rapidly away from city centers, constructing large reservoirs to reduce precipitation variability—often creates many new and unintended problems. By defining problems more broadly, it is possible to come up with more holistic, comprehensive solutions as well. In all cases, moving forward with NBS with clients should reflect a joint desire to meet client needs in ways that are cost-effective, useful, appropriate, and sustainable.

(iii) Would ADB partners be willing to include NBS options during project development?

By including NBS as part of the range of options open to clients, it is possible to create a wide-ranging palette of options, which can span from traditional gray solutions to green ecosystem-based approaches. Most of the shades in that palette of solutions, however, will be between dark gray and bright green: they will be hybrid solutions that integrate, stage, or merge green and gray in intermediate shades. As examples, a reservoir may include groundwater storage to increase capacity, while a roadway may use a mixture of local, native plants with constructed drainage to prevent erosion. Working across the spectrum of gray and green should be a significant goal in all of our work.

(iv) Are ADB partners willing to consider including co-benefits when considering performance?

NBS often provide co-benefits such as the improvement of livelihoods, fisheries, recreation, and the creation of green jobs (Raymond et al. 2017). However, important questions remain about how to assess the impacts of NBS within and across different societal challenges. When fulfilling the functions of urban infrastructures using or mimicking natural processes, NBS may simultaneously provide co-benefits for biodiversity and human well-being. Examples of different types of indicators for assessing the impacts of NBS across different challenge areas are shown in Table 3.

Table 3: Examples of Nature-Based Solutions Co-Benefit Categories

Challenge Area	Example of Indicator	Type of Indicator	Unit of Measurement
	Net carbon sequestration by urban forests (including GHG emissions from maintenance activities)	Environmental (chemical)	tC per ha/year
	Economic benefit of reduction of stormwater to be treated in public sewerage system	Economic (monetary)	Cost of sewerage treatment by volume (€/m^3)
	Area remaining for erosion protection	Environmental (physical)	km^2 or m^2
	Species richness of indigenous vegetation	Environmental (physical)	A count, magnitude, or intensity score of indigenous species per unit area
	Annual amount of pollutants captured by vegetation	Environmental (chemical)	t pollutant per ha/year
	Index of ecological connectivity (integral index of connectivity)	Enviromental (physical)	Probability that two dispersers randomly located in a landscape can reach each other
	Quality of the participatory or governance processes	Social (process)	Perceived level of trust, legitimacy, transparency, and accountability of process
	Accessibility to public green space	Social (justice)	% of people living within a given distance from accessible, public green space
	Level of involvement in frequent pysical activity in urban green spaces	Social (physiological)	Number and % of people being physically active (minimum of 30 minutes, 3 times per week) in urban green spaces
	Net additional jobs in the green sector enabled by NBS projects	Economic (productivity)	New jobs/specific green sector/year

C = carbon, GHG = greenhouse gas, ha = hectare, km^2 = square kilometer, m^2 = square meter, m^3 = cubic meter, NBS = nature-based solution, t = ton.
Source: C. Raymond et al. 2017. A Framework for Assessing and Implementing the Co-Benefits of Nature-Based Solutions in Urban Areas. *Environmental Science & Policy*. 77. pp. 15–24. https://doi.org/10.1016/j.envsci.2017.07.008.

NBS targeted toward a specific societal challenge is likely to produce co-benefits as well as costs and neutral effects in other challenges. For example, flood peak reduction actions designed with nature in mind are likely to have co-benefits for not only coastal resilience, but also for quality of life by improving urban living conditions. Improving environmental qualities and the related increase of property values, however, can adversely affect social justice and social cohesion by contributing to gentrification.

4. Help clients understand their options.

In many cases, ADB staff and DMC partners will be developing and choosing NBS options from a palette of colors. The following list of qualities for three broad categories can help give some insight into how, when, and why particular choices from that palette may be most appropriate to the project needs and context.

(i) Traditional gray projects

- Project success is not at all contingent on ecological outcomes and impacts;
- Environmental impact assessment focuses on immediate area of the project;
- Environmental impact assessment only spans short temporal period;
- Narrow project definition;

- Highly optimized design and operations, with limited regard to environmental and climatic uncertainties;
- Constructed, especially with nonlocal, highly manufactured materials;
- Operated without regard to natural processes or cycles;
- Built and/or operated without regard to ecosystems that are or may be impacted; and
- Environmental regulatory and monitoring systems are weak and not enforced.

Note: Pure gray projects may be appropriate when the following conditions are present:

- There is a need for high certainty around technical performance (e.g., structural properties and operation and maintenance characteristics);
- Narrow and well-understood scope of operation or operating conditions (i.e., range of input parameters to which the infrastructure is subject is limited and well-understood); and
- Narrow and confined impacts (i.e., relatively limited project with well-understood and predicable impacts on the environment).

Gray infrastructure tends to be optimized around one to two performance criteria, but poorly suited to dealing with complex problems and interactions, and relatively inflexible or not adaptive. In this sense, gray is narrowly "strong" but broadly "fragile."

(ii) Greener gray and green–gray hybrid projects

- Project success is contingent on low impact;
- Include environmental co-benefit values;
- Environmental impact assessment spans the operational life span of investment (e.g., 50–100 years);
- Spatial impact analysis extends well beyond the project site (e.g., catchment, upstream–downstream relationships, basin, movement or transfer of ecosystem services);
- Design incorporates aspects of the local landscape and ecological processes;
- Environmental performance monitoring systems inform decision-making, regulations; and
- Ecosystem processes covered by governance processes that are transparent can be regulated and/or enforced.

(iii) Greenest projects

- Project success is contingent on integration of ecosystem and ecosystem services resilience;
- Explicitly incorporate environmental co-benefits and services into project evaluation and operations;
- Environmental impact assessment spans beyond the operational life span of investment (e.g., what could come after?);
- Existing landscapes are restored, enhanced, and protected;
- Operations adjust to and reflect natural processes, systems, variability, and change;
- Governance incorporates reevaluation processes that update operations with increasing knowledge of climate trends, including regulatory and enforcement processes; and
- Operations and design are managed for climatic and ecological resilience.

Note: Green may be more appropriate when there is some range of tolerance for infrastructure performance (larger safety margins). Input parameters and operating conditions involve a lot of complex variables. The interactions are not well-understood since these need an inherent adaptive and reflexive capacity from the infrastructure (i.e., resilience to unexpected or unforeseen shocks).

Green can be narrowly suboptimal in performance, compared to gray, but much more resilient to a broader set of unforeseen circumstances. Impacts of the infrastructure could be wide ranging and complex and we are unable to reliably predict them. Where there is a risk of localized environmental or ecological tipping points, NBS offer a "tread lightly" and lower-risk investment under these circumstances.

4.   Strategies to Overcome Objections

Caution is a natural response to new ideas, especially if your colleagues have difficulty imagining the project proceeding through his or her institution, serving in situ, or providing the intended services. If you have worked through some or all the client's NBS checklist, then you should have a good sense of the set of experiences and perspectives that your partners possess toward NBS.

With reluctant (or potentially reluctant) adopters, one of the safest strategies for building support is to suggest that in the project design stage, explore and compare a spectrum of solutions. More details will be provided in Chapters 4 and 5 about how to structure and develop the spectrum, but many clients may be more comfortable if adding green and hybrid options does not also mean that traditional gray solutions have been eliminated as potential choices.

Even so, clients may remain skeptical. Several responses may be effective to consider as you move forward into program and project development to help overcome real or potential objections when clients appear cautious about NBS options:

1.   **Organize a study tour with key client staff to see similar projects that are already functioning.**

Ideally, such a project is in the same or a similar peer country, but partners will also benefit from seeing NBS in context in more developed countries (e.g., Japan, Singapore, or even Australia or those in Europe). It will also help to be familiar with the stories of specific successful NBS so that you can understand the art of the possible and share it with partners. Here are two examples of the experience of the Netherlands and London.

The Netherlands Sand Engine

The sand engine on the Dutch coast is a new ecosystem.[4] It is an innovative coastal management design that was planned and implemented to prevent the erosion of a section of the Dutch coastline, exploiting the flow of existing local coastal currents.

Multiple benefits: In the context of restoring the local ecosystem, the sand engine enhances and offers better protection to biodiversity (i.e., local marine and shoreline species), securing local habitat, and food provision. Additionally, it promotes the sustainable development of the coastal area while ensuring climate adaptation, risk management, and resilience. The project is designed in such a way that it generates additional benefits for nature development, recreation, and knowledge development (societal benefits) too.

London: Nature-Based Solutions for a Leading Sustainable City

London has planned and implemented several NBS to address multiple climate- and urbanization-related challenges. These include green roofs and walls, planting street trees, expanding or improving green spaces, urban agriculture, natural water retention measures, and the recycling of derelict areas, brownfields, and other urban land.[5]

Multiple benefits: The London NBS aims to transform the city into a green capital via reduction of surface water flooding, improved air quality, urban cooling, walking and cycling opportunities, and aesthetic improvements, including enhancing biodiversity and ecological resilience (Mayor of London 2016). In this case, NBS do not only enhance biodiversity and sustainability but also contribute to climate mitigation through carbon storage, as well as reduced heat stress and flood risks. Lastly, the case of London proves that multiple benefits can also be achieved when restoring brownfield sites or constructing green roofs.

---

4   Oppla. Delft Sand Engine. https://oppla.eu/casestudy/17630.
5   Oppla. London-NBS for a Leading Sustainable City. https://oppla.eu/casestudy/19456.

2. **Conduct capacity-building workshops with technical staff to build expertise and raise expectations for implementing nature-based solutions.**

    Particularly for professional and operational staff, hands-on exercises can ensure that the project minimizes conflict and surprises, and that it can be managed and operated by the client.

3. **Identify co-benefits.**

    An alternative approach to overcoming objections is finding how NBS can solve multiple problems, concerns, or development challenges facing a client. Often the process of identifying co-benefits is unfamiliar to partners and clients and they require some imaginative support.

    It will be helpful to provide evidence that similar NBS meet performance expectations at an effective cost–benefit ratio while also providing co-benefits. Often, co-benefits are important for high-level decision-makers, politicians, and when community and civil society groups are involved in decision-making. Sometimes, surprising allies may be found, such as store owners who believe property values may rise more rapidly when a more attractive green project rather than a gray solution is implemented, or fishers who may see increasing habitat and greater potential catches from a more natural setting.

    Co-benefits are also critical if ADB staff will choose a multicriteria analysis (MCA) approach instead of the more traditional cost–benefit analysis (CBA) approach to project justification (Chapter 5). In comparison to CBA, MCA is not a costing approach but rather a qualitative assessment of different options using a range of criteria that could potentially be weighted. MCAs are generally comparative evaluations that measure potential options against predetermined criteria. They make the options and their contributions against the criteria explicit and generally involve a relative weighting system.

    The weight attached to a criterion would depend on the stakeholders ranking the options such as the community, industry, and government. In some rare cases, there is a quantitative assessment of a particular criterion (i.e., for climate change, carbon dioxide emissions may be used) but, ultimately, the assessment and ranking will be qualitative in nature (low, medium, high; or color-coded; or numbered 1, 2, 3, etc.). Working with clients early in the strategy or prefeasibility stage to identify potential benefits and allies to garner support to maintain NBS options is important.

    Some examples of categories of co-benefits are included in Table 3, but just as important is the process of trying to look for synergies between ministries and in defining a larger problem shed that may create opportunities for multipurpose projects with more comprehensive solutions.

4. **Show how gray solutions can have unintended side effects.**

    An example of this is the public backlash from reduced access to natural areas and green space that results in a lower quality of life within the community. Nearby communities may serve as an outgroup and contrast: "We can do better here and avoid these mistakes."

5. **Talk about how many developed countries have shifted away from relying only on gray infrastructure to include a broader range of infrastructure options, as necessary and appropriate.**

    Indeed, many developed countries have even reached a stage where they are removing gray investments in favor of NBS. As a result, developing countries can leap ahead in development without the middle step of investing in infrastructure that will not age well or infrastructure with negative and unappealing side effects that are difficult or impossible to reverse.

IV Developing an Upstream Nature-Based Solutions Strategy

Greener approaches to economic development for water, transport, and cities are increasing in implementation and in acceptance. But for most institutions, nature-based solutions (NBS) remain unusual pilot or experimental projects, often growing outside of normal project development guidelines, sometimes with exceptional rules applied to them. Mainstreaming, in this context, means normalizing green and hybrid solutions within existing decision-making processes, such that NBS are seen as comparable, if not competitive, alternatives to traditional infrastructure investments. This chapter will discuss opportunities within ADB processes to increase the number of NBS entering the project pipeline.

Mainstreaming must also include alignment with higher priorities and agendas. At ADB, NBS align well with recent high-level institutional strategy. Strategy 2030 sets out environmental sustainability as one of the priorities, notably Operational Priority 3: Tackling Climate Change, Building Climate and Disaster Resilience, and Enhancing Environmental Sustainability. The operational plan provides the following environment-related focus areas: (i) environmental management, including pollution control; (ii) natural capital investments (e.g., NBS); and (iii) environmental governance, such as through policy and legal reforms and market-based approaches.

This chapter will look at how broad programmatic and country strategies can be aligned with NBS, to ensure that greener approaches can be explored and ultimately implemented at the project level.

1. Incorporating Green Approaches into ADB Projects: A Process Approach

NBS are certainly the oldest approaches to how humans, as a species, have pursued economic development. Archeological evidence suggests that artificial wetlands, for instance, were being created for rice agriculture in the PRC at least 7,000 years ago. However, these early NBS projects probably did not need to go through complex and bureaucratic project development, design, and finance approval processes before beginning implementation.

Although ADB is only some 5 decades old, the institution's systems were implicitly designed to promote projects that fit a traditional gray profile. This guide assumes that the overall decision-making process within ADB should not see radical changes to support the implementation of NBS. Instead, this guide works to adjust existing ADB processes so that greener interventions are more acceptable, can be compared more readily to traditional solutions, and are likely to successfully reach implementation.

2. Creating National-Level Strategic Buy-In: Country Partnership Strategy

While increasing the possibilities for NBS at a project scale are important, in many cases, engaging client acceptance at a national level can enlarge the range of options and situations relevant to NBS before shifting to defining specific projects. A country partnership strategy (CPS), which is updated every 5 years, can serve as a platform to develop a basis with clients to explore NBS-relevant solutions (Figure 2).

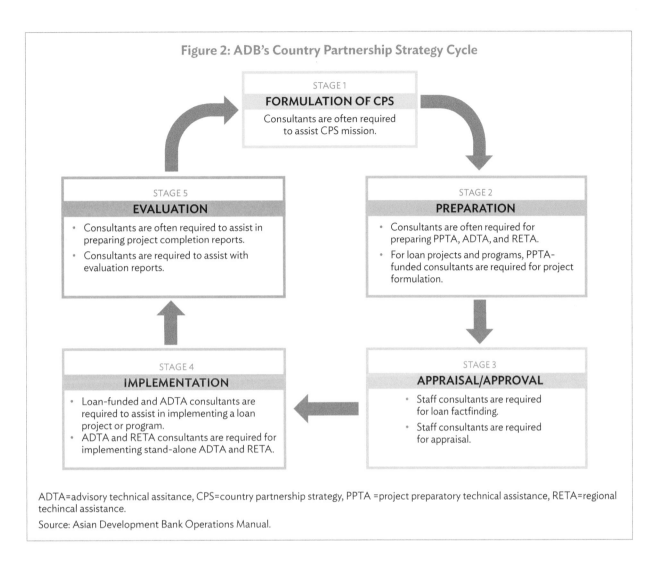

Figure 2: ADB's Country Partnership Strategy Cycle

STAGE 1
FORMULATION OF CPS
Consultants are often required
to assist CPS mission.

STAGE 5
EVALUATION
- Consultants are often required to assist in preparing project completion reports.
- Consultants are required to assist with evaluation reports.

STAGE 2
PREPARATION
- Consultants are often required for preparing PPTA, ADTA, and RETA.
- For loan projects and programs, PPTA-funded consultants are required for project formulation.

STAGE 4
IMPLEMENTATION
- Loan-funded and ADTA consultants are required to assist in implementing a loan project or program.
- ADTA and RETA consultants are required for implementing stand-alone ADTA and RETA.

STAGE 3
APPRAISAL/APPROVAL
- Staff consultants are required for loan factfinding.
- Staff consultants are required for appraisal.

ADTA=advisory technical assitance, CPS=country partnership strategy, PPTA =project preparatory technical assistance, RETA=regional techincal assistance.
Source: Asian Development Bank Operations Manual.

Updating a CPS is led by ADB resident missions. The resident missions coordinate and discuss with their respective governments those critical environmental and related issues and opportunities in the developing member countries (DMCs). A CPS that explicitly identifies NBS as a key modality for investment and project development can influence many projects conceived over the whole funding period and create windows of opportunity for green solutions through two key modalities:

(i)   framing the critical issues that a DMC faces where ADB can provide influence and support, and

(ii) defining a set of potential solutions to address them effectively and efficiently.

A strategic advisory service can support upstream analytical work and policy dialogue in the preparation of updates to the CPS. Revisions to the CPS are a prime opportunity for ADB to introduce NBS within the range of effective solutions with clients. Especially with topics such as climate change adaptation (CCA) and disaster risk management (DRM) programs, numerous examples exist of effective interventions in both areas. An advisory service should include

(i)   assessing critical environmental issues and opportunities in the DMCs through, for example, country environment note (CEN) and/or strategic environmental assessment;

(ii) prioritized key environmental issues and corresponding interventions in the CPS;

(iii) consultation with operations departments and resident missions to prioritize the solutions and prepare options for investments and TA;

(iv) participation in and contribution to a national or regional policy dialogue, as necessary;

(v)   an issues paper and/or an inclusive and sustainable growth assessment, with recommendations for priority solutions or options in the CPS;

(vi)   drafting of a CPS from the inclusive and sustainable growth assessment and/or issues paper, which is followed by a country operations business plan and/or indicative country pipeline and monitoring; and

(vii)   the identification and design of pipeline investment and TA projects, with priority interventions based on the country operations business plan and/or indicative country pipeline monitoring.

The resident mission circulates these documents to different departments for feedback. The Environment Thematic Group comments on the two documents and releases a CEN. A CEN highlights environmental recommendations that should be considered in the CPS. Later in this chapter, guidance for aligning a CPS with regional, national, and global policy initiatives related to both DRM and CCA is presented.

3.   Aligning Nature-Based Solutions with Key ADB Priorities and Programs: Climate Change Adaptation and Disaster Risk Management

NBS can provide essential support and advantages to ADB's Strategy 2030 Operational Priorities. NBS do not represent a separate, additional agenda but a new set of options to help better meet existing programmatic and client needs. Table 4 shows how NBS can support ADB operational priorities.

In keeping with these emerging opportunities, ADB has chosen to align NBS with two intertwined programs. DRM is a long-standing approach for securing the development of Asia and the Pacific economies. On the other hand, CCA is a relatively newer body of approaches, many of which are still evolving, to cope with realized and emerging climate impacts. CCA has recently been prioritized as a critical investment area by ADB leadership (ADB 2018). ADB has also recently been mainstreaming climate risk assessment and risk reduction within the ADB portfolio while also developing an active program to implement projects that are designed to build community and economic resilience (Watkiss, Wilby, and Rodgers 2020).

Table 4: How Nature-Based Solutions Can Support ADB Operational Priorities

ADB Operational Priority	How NBS Can Support	Example/Reference
Addressing remaining poverty and reducing inequalities	NBS ensure that natural capital reserves are protected, restored, and enhanced for future generations, creating broader stakeholder engagement through inclusive processes. In many cases, NBS can be scaled up cost effectively, creating more comprehensive and larger scale solutions that also integrate communities into their operation and management.	Integration with protected areas, soil and water conservation, supporting livelihoods
Tackling climate change, building climate and disaster resilience, and enhancing environmental sustainability	NBS often have inherent flexibility to cope with climate uncertainty. NBS can also support climate mitigation by sequestering atmospheric carbon in soils, wetlands, and coastal regions.	Water-related efforts[a] Inclusion of Wetlands into Nationally Determined Contributions[b]

continued on next page

Table 4 *continued*

ADB Operational Priority	How NBS Can Support	Example/Reference
Promoting rural development and food security	MAR can capture floodwaters and convert into dry-season irrigation storage.	Using Flood Water for Managed Aquifer Recharge to Support Sustainable Water Resources[c]
Fostering regional cooperation and integration	"Room for the river" flood risk reduction approaches create coordinated regional approach between upstream and downstream areas.	Improving Governance in Transboundary Cooperation in Water and Climate Change Adaptation[d]
Accelerating progress in gender equality	NBS can support more enduring, resilient clean water and hygiene systems in rural areas.	Sand dams in East Africa create local water storage and retrieval system, especially for women in rural communities[e]
Making cities more livable	Both flood and drought risk can be managed by working with larger agricultural landscapes and creating flood absorption wetlands zones within cities.	Jiangxi Pingxiang Integrated Rural–Urban Infrastructure Development (Appendix 1) Udon Thani, Thailand[f]
Strengthening governance and institutional capacity	NBS often require a formal legal, governance, and regulatory mechanism to enable finance and management.	Water funds can represent ecosystem services within governance frameworks.[g]

ADB = Asian Development Bank, MAR = managed aquifer recharge, NBS = nature-based solution.

[a] D. M. Smith et al. 2019. *Adaptation's Thirst: Accelerating the Convergence of Water and Climate Action*. Background Paper prepared for the 2019 report of the Global Commission on Adaptation. Rotterdam and Washington, DC.

[b] N. F. Anisha et al. 2020. *Locking Carbon in Wetlands: Enhancing Climate Action by Including Wetlands in NDCs*. Corvallis, Oregon and Wageningen, The Netherlands: Alliance for Global Water Adaptation and Wetlands International.

[c] Government of the United States, California Department of Water Resources. 2017. *FLOOD-MAR: Using Flood Water for Managed Aquifer Recharge to Support Sustainable Water Resources*. California.

[d] J. Timmerman et al. 2017. Improving Governance in Transboundary Cooperation in Water and Climate Change Adaptation. *Water Policy*. 19 (6). pp. 1014–1029.

[e] S. Maddrell and I. Neal. 2012. *Sand Dams: A Practical Guide*. London.

[f] G. Mendoza et al. 2018. *Climate Risk Informed Decision Analysis (CRIDA): Collaborative Water Resources Planning for an Uncertain Future*. Paris: UNESCO Publishing.

[g] K. Brauman et al. 2019. Water Funds. In L. A. Mandle et al., eds. *Green Growth That Works*. Washington, DC: Island Press. pp. 118–140.

Source: ADB. 2020. *Protecting and Investing in Natural Capital in Asia and the Pacific: A Practitioner's Guide to Nature-Based Solutions*. Consultant's report. Manila (TA 9461-REG). https://www.adb.org/sites/default/files/project-documents/50159/50159-001-tacr-en_3.pdf.

Both CCA and DRM program areas have strong interconnections as well, given that many DRM investments are intended to address extreme weather events such as droughts and floods, which are themselves subject to the influence of additional climate change. NBS offer significant opportunities for both CCA and DRM, as described in Table 5.

Table 5: Contribution of Nature-Based Solutions to
Climate Change Adaptation and Disaster Risk Management Programs

NBS Contributions to CCA and DRM	Contribution in Practice
Slow-onset hazards	Building on functions that can buffer extreme events such as droughts, groundwater saline intrusion, and erosion. Capturing stormwaters for groundwater recharge, managed aquifer pumping, vegetated banks to capture and hold water and soil.
Fast-onset hazards	Intense storm events, "rain bombs," and flash flooding require NBS that can prevent or reduce risk in advance as well as defer or deflect extreme and damaging flows, such as a "room for the river" approach.
Building resilience	NBS are especially strong in creating redundancy, flexibility, robustness, and inclusiveness. The ecological connectedness that is inherent to NBS allows them to be self-healing and self-maintaining in many cases.
Cost-effectiveness	NBS often have lower installation and construction costs and can also build wealth. Aligning ecosystems with existing institutions and livelihoods can create a broad institutional buy-in with ongoing political benefits and support.
	NBS often increase property values by indirectly creating economic investment zones that foster pride, community engagement, and multipurpose uses, such as the green growth zones in Hue, Viet Nam.

CCA = climate change adaptation, DRM = disaster risk management, NBS = nature-based solutions.
Source: Authors.

In terms of CCA, ADB now distinguishes between projects that need to be climate proofed and those whose primary purpose is climate change adaptation. Projects that will be climate proofed are not primarily addressing a climate impact or impacts. Instead, they need to cope with some climate change risks and be able to operate at acceptable performance levels in the face of ongoing impacts. Some options and strategies are discussed later in this chapter.

NBS are widely hailed right now for their efficacy with CCA. However, the main intent of the investment is to take advantage of or reduce the influence of climate impacts now and in the future. In many cases, these claims can come across as advocacy rather than as based on evidence. NBS do not naturally provide climate adaptation or climate resilience benefits without justification and probably not often without design. This is also true for gray infrastructure. Effective climate adaptation needs some planning and strategy. The basis for a higher level of justification is described below.

The most significant argument in favor of NBS for both CCA and DRM is that ecosystems are more flexible than gray infrastructure. That is, they can often be expanded, altered, adjusted, or even removed more easily than traditional investments. As such, they may be especially appropriate in concert with gray infrastructure, such as in areas in which there is a higher tolerance for failure, such as agricultural flooding rather than central city flooding. Given the uncertainties associated with ongoing and future climate impacts and the appearance of unforeseen extreme events, flexible investments offer an effective strategy for modifying investments over time.

4. Nature-Based Solutions and Risk Assessment

Many peer institutions are evolving in their approaches to CCA and DRM for assessing risk with NBS projects. Moreover, while ecosystems can indeed provision climate resilience, often these same ecosystems will need active climate adaptation interventions themselves (Poff et al. 2016; Matthews et al. 2019)—i.e., it is not correct to assume that adaptation benefits will automatically flow from the incorporation of ecosystems within climate adaptation plans or that realized benefits will persist without active management. Ecological resilience is normally a choice and should be planned for (Brown et al. 2019; Grantham, Matthews, and Bledsoe 2019).

A critical aspect for exploring the relationship of any project at ADB to climate change is through a climate risk and adaptation assessment (CRA). This assessment process has been well-defined at ADB, although some aspects of the CRA are more appropriate for traditional infrastructure investments than for examining the climate risks that ecosystems may be exposed to or that they may mitigate. As with DRM projects (described below), the use of NBS will be more positive and likely using a system-level understanding of major drivers, probably at a basin or catchment scale. Ideally, this understanding is developed at the concept stage.

In 2019, ADB updated the institutional CRA process to support the increasing emphasis on climate adaptation within the overall investment portfolio (ADB 2020). The new methodology looks at two major topics: (i) the level of detail and effort necessary to evaluate climate risk (Figure 3), and the primary intended purpose of the investment (Table 6).

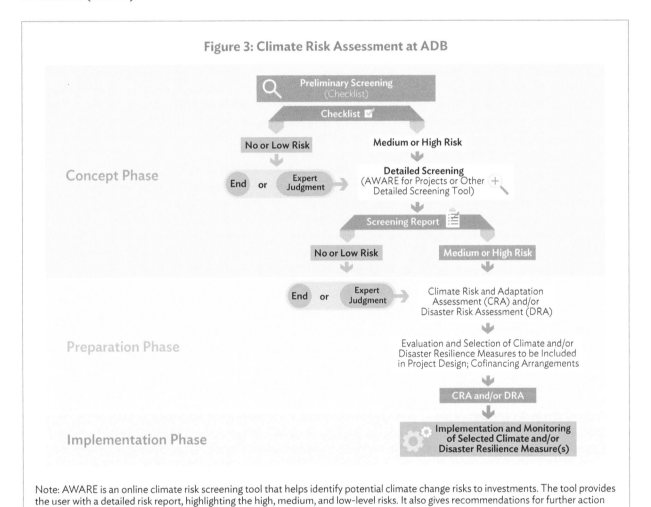

Figure 3: Climate Risk Assessment at ADB

Note: AWARE is an online climate risk screening tool that helps identify potential climate change risks to investments. The tool provides the user with a detailed risk report, highlighting the high, medium, and low-level risks. It also gives recommendations for further action (Acclimatise. 2018. AWARE for Projects: Fast, Comprehensive Climate Risk Screening).

Source: Asian Development Bank.

Table 6: Type 1 and Type 2 Climate Change Projects

Type of Project	Detailed CRA	Light-Touch CRA	NBS Implication
Type 1: Climate Proofing *Climate adaptation is a secondary objective.*	New large hydroelectric power plant and reservoir: *long lifetime, high risk of lock-in, high level of precaution and safety required, large investment*	Upgrade of existing road project or new wind power project: *shorter lifetime, low risk of lock-in, low level of precaution, small investment*	Most NBS projects that target transport should be Type 1 projects. Hybrid projects that include both gray and green components will more likely require a detailed CRA. Unless quite large, projects that are more substantially NBS should only require a light-touch approach.
Type 2: Adaptation *Climate adaptation is the principal objective.*	New hard coastal protection to defend against sea-level risks: *principal objective, long lifetime* New building codes or engineering design standards that incorporate allowances for climate change: *principal objective, risk of sector lock-in*	Some technical assistance projects, policy reform, and resilience financing: *principal objective, but short lifetime, with a focus on enabling conditions for in-depth adaptation*	Most water-related projects, including urban resilience projects, will be Type 2 projects. Investments that combine gray and green elements, including some types of resource management policy loans (e.g., land use change, agriculture) may also fall into this category. Most other NBS projects will be better served as light-touch approaches.

CRA = climate risk and adaptation assessment, NBS = nature-based solution.
Source: P. Watkiss, R. Wilby, and C. A. Rodgers. 2020. Principles of Climate Risk Management for Climate Proofing Projects. *ADB Sustainable Development Working Paper Series*. No. 69. Manila: Asian Development Bank. http://dx.doi.org/10.22617/WPS200203-2.

The purpose of the investment is an important issue for consideration in the new ADB approach to climate risk. All projects are categorized as either Type 1 or Type 2, referring to the major intent of the investment:

1. **Type 1 projects focus on traditional ADB sector categories such as transport, irrigation, or wastewater treatment.**

   They do not have a primary focus on climate adaptation and addressing climate impacts. As such, the type of CRA necessary is now referred to as climate proofing, which in most cases will be "light touch"—unless the CRA reveals significant risk and exposure, and a more thorough analysis is necessary. Currently, most ADB investments fall into this category. Typical adaptation options in these cases are likely to emphasize so-called "low-regret" options, "overbuilding" for robust designs, and designing for shorter operational lifetimes so that the project can be adjusted, updated, recommissioned, or reoperationalized over time. Both physical and "soft" (behavioral, operational, or governance) options should be considered. If climate risks are low relative to other drivers, no adaptation efforts may be necessary at all.

2. **Type 2 projects emphasize adaptation benefits.**

   The burden of proof necessary for documenting adaptation is higher for these projects, and, as a result, their CRA is more detailed and thorough. In many cases, the higher burden of proof reflects ADB and broader donor-led and multilateral development bank-led efforts to track climate finance. Type 2 investments are rapidly expanding as a category within ADB and can be expected to form a significant pillar of ADB investments in the future. Adaptation options can include those described above, as well as more direct and active approaches such as adjusting the design, operations, and governance plans to cover a broader range of potential futures.

In both cases, the new recommendations suggest beginning with an initial screening tool—currently AWARE for Projects, though this may change with time (Acclimatise 2018)—and a greater emphasis on looking at current and inherent systemic risks (sometimes referred to as a bottom–up risk assessment methodology) rather than on evaluating risks primarily through extrinsic sources of climate data, such as circulation models (sometimes referred to as a top–down assessment methodology) (Garcia et al. 2014). It is strongly suggested to address climate risks and opportunities early in the project cycle, as well as more broadly within the client and partner relationship (e.g., through the CPS revision process; Chapter 4).

Although NBS are not mentioned in the new methodology (ADB 2020), the relevance of NBS to these recommendations seems clear—i.e., projects that emphasize NBS over gray and hybrid components are light-touch projects, regardless of their nominal purpose. NBS generally have a strong inherent ability to prevent lock-in errors; as such, NBS are often chosen for their ability to retain flexibility in the face of uncertainty (Matthews et al. 2019). For large investments, especially those that substantially combine or emphasize gray infrastructure components, more intensive and thorough CRAs should be explored.

As with CRA, risk assessment for DRM follows a clear methodology at ADB. Figure 4 illustrates how disaster risk assessments, and their outputs and recommendations, can fit into ADB's project management cycle—particularly into the concept, project design, and project preparatory TA processes—to strengthen disaster resilience.

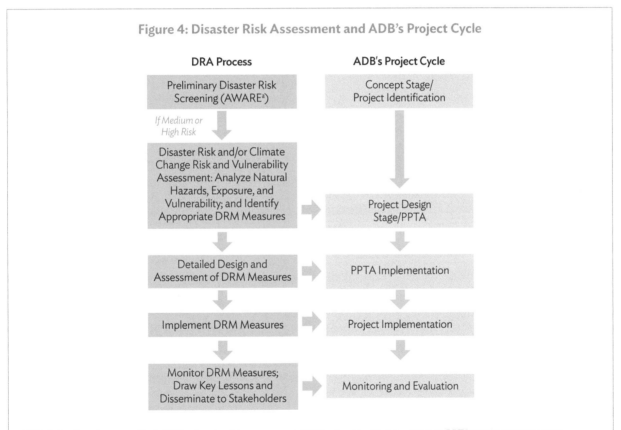

Figure 4: Disaster Risk Assessment and ADB's Project Cycle

ADB=Asian Development Bank, DRA=disaster risk assessment, DRM=disaster risk management, PPTA=project preparatory technical assistance.

a   AWARE is an online climate risk screening tool that helps identify potential climate change risks to investments. The tool provides the user with a detailed risk report, highlighting the high, medium, and low-level risks. It also gives recommendations for further action (Acclimatise. 2018. *AWARE for Projects: Fast, Comprehensive Climate Risk Screening*).

Source: ADB. 2017. *Disaster Risk Assessment for Project Preparation: A Practical Guide*. Manila. http://dx.doi.org/10.22617/TIM178893-2.

NBS are relevant at all stages of the disaster risk assessment process. But in the preliminary screening process, NBS may be most important by developing a systems-level understanding of drivers and the range of potential solutions that may be relevant and useful to consider. For instance, urban flood risk may be more easily managed far upstream, such as in agro-ecological landscapes, by altering the rate and direction of water movement through the basin (International Hydropower Association 2019).

5.   Aligning Climate Change Adaptation and Nature-Based Solutions at National Levels

In this context, we define climate adaptation as interventions that are intended to respond to already realized or potential climate impacts. According to ADB guidelines and standard practices, CCA projects should be designed as a response to one or more explicitly identified climate impacts, which is having an influence now and/or will in the future. At the program or country strategy level, this means that at least a climate change influence on an issue should be identified even if a climate risk and vulnerability analysis has not been completed yet, since climate vulnerability analysis typically occurs on a project basis.

Such a standard is not difficult to meet in most cases, especially since in a CPS, or national adaptation plan (NAP), the intent is to identify broad patterns instead of individual projects. If directly climate-related events such as droughts, floods, and intense precipitation; intense storms including typhoons; groundwater management; hillside, riparian, or coastal erosion; or extreme air temperatures are identified as important gaps, then climate change is almost certainly involved in current conditions (with a growing impact for the future). Indirect impacts also tend to have a strong climate linkage, such as irrigation (to reduce climate variability), sea level rise, damage to transport systems and networks, urban heat island effects, coping with crop pests and low crop productivity, and protecting sensitive communities, protected areas, and infrastructure assets.

Making strategic references to NBS in high-level planning documents can help ensure that green options are developed and seriously considered as plans evolve into adaptation projects. Gray infrastructure usually has immediate, measurable impacts and is particularly effective in reducing the impacts of specific hazards over the short term.

Nonetheless, these investments are often expensive, very focused in terms of deliverable benefits, and deliver very few, if any, co-benefits; whereas, NBS are usually more affordable, provide a wide range of ecosystem services, and offer protection from multiple hazards—which is important because hazards seldom occur in isolation and mostly take place simultaneously or in a cascade.

For example, mangrove forest along a coastline can provide protection from coastal flooding and erosion, strong winds, and high temperatures. It can also provide a range of ecosystem services and support diverse livelihood options. Contrary to engineered approaches, NBS also involve and benefit local communities, can be more adaptive to new conditions, and are less likely to create a false sense of security since they sustain over a longer span of time. Hence, NBS are very suitable as a CCA approach (Seddon 2018).

Developing a CCA NBS strategy is more straightforward than just a few years ago. The 2015 UNFCCC Paris Agreement created a new national policy instrument called a Nationally Determined Contribution (NDC), which contains prominent CCA and climate mitigation (carbon emissions reduction and carbon sequestration and storage) components. For many countries, the NDCs have the potential to become an important contributor and parallel document to the ADB CPS. In the future, CPS should refer to draft or finalized NDC programs, sectors, and issues.

Each country submits their NDCs, which are structured as 5-year plans. The first formal NDCs are due for submission at the 2021 United Nations Climate Change Conference (or more commonly referred to as COP26), scheduled in November 2021. In most cases, the NDCs are managed and coordinated by the environment ministries, though some variation exists here as well. The UNFCCC requests each country to name both climate mitigation and climate adaptation focal points.

As new policy instruments, the NDCs are still evolving, and the UNFCCC has only provided general guidance on how to structure the NDCs. That said, the NDCs are typically short documents (10–20 pages) that outline a broad set of issues, sectors, and key actors for adaptation and mitigation. The NDCs are widely expected to be important vehicles for how donors and other funding sources identify and prioritize climate finance of the 5-year term of each NDC. Countries are expected to revise their NDCs into the future through these 5-year intervals.

Except for smaller countries (e.g., Pacific island countries and territories), the NDCs rarely drop to the level of describing specific projects. ADB staff should also note that focal point staff do not typically manage individual projects. Indeed, beyond very small countries, the national government may have little or no role on many of the programs identified in an NDC, nor does the ministry coordinating the NDC even when the national government is involved.

Thus, an energy project may not have a close connection to the environment ministry staff, though the NDC focal point would need to track the project for the UNFCCC reporting. For adaptation projects, many subnational entities are likely to be important. Cities or broader regional urban networks may be important at both national, provincial, and local scales.

Transportation and urban resilience projects may also be framed primarily as climate mitigation projects with adaptation components, such as low-carbon mass transit with adaptation or wildlife-friendly elements. Although less common, some water utility and wastewater or fecal sludge projects may also have linked mitigation–adaptation components while remaining within a larger water sector category. The potential for gaps in interministerial and multilevel governance coordination is high for the NDCs, especially as they begin to coalesce as more fully operational areas of policy.

DRM programs are also widespread components of the NDCs, especially in countries affected by typhoons or those with have high levels of climate variability and have many extreme events (droughts and floods). DRM and CCA are often closely aligned in adaptation priorities, and for the NDCs, there may not be a clear distinction between hazard categories.

For ADB staff, these policy issues have, more generally, important implications for ADB programs and CPS. How a project is labeled can have implications for the scope of funding and range of partners who are involved. Following are issues to be aware of in this regard:

(i)   Even other environment ministry staff may have little or no awareness of relevant NDC provisions. Hence, it is important to seek out the relevant NDC while developing the CPS and when developing more general CCA and DRM program priorities to ensure alignment.

(ii)   Creating a program-level relationship with the relevant national adaptation focal point may be useful for both ongoing coordination, as well as influencing future iterations of the CPS and NDC.

(iii) Concessional support and capacity building are increasingly available for the NDCs, especially at the sector level and in the crosscutting role of specific types of interventions, such as water and NBS. Organizations such as the NDC Partnership and the Global Center on Adaptation, for instance, are designed to ensure efficacy and coordination. The Global Center on Adaptation's action tracks, for instance, specifically focus on NBS approaches to a variety of sector interventions for adaptation.

(iv) Because the NDCs are written at a national level, they can sometimes make connections across sectors more readily than individual ministries. Irrigation, flood control, and urban resilience may all be priority areas that would be amenable to a small number of complementary NBS. However, the relevant ministries or other administrative entities may have difficulty seeing beyond their mandate. An NDC may help spark efforts to find synergies.

For DMCs, NAPs will also be relevant to ADB strategies. NAPs may or may not be led by the same person as the NDC adaptation focal point. NAPs are an older UNFCCC policy instrument, and they typically go into more project-level details, especially for extreme events that can be influenced by climate change. The NAP Global Network has proven to be an important resource, ensuring that NAPs bridge gaps between finance and projects, as well as finding synergies between NAPs and NDCs. NAPs have been around for more than a decade and are explicitly designed to guide donor funding and concessional finance sources.

As older instruments, NAPs may have a less sophisticated approach to adaptation, and many older NAPs make little or no reference to NBS. However, NAPs can at least provide some sense of where CCA and DRM issues can inform a CPS. They often include some national-level climate risk and hazard assessment, at least in terms of broad climate patterns and potential sector risks. For some funding sources such as the Global Environment Facility and the Green Climate Fund, NAPs have long served as a basis for defining and pursuing in-country program priorities.

Climate adaptation investments are here to stay. Their most important element for ADB strategy is an explicit link to climate impacts and, ideally, these investments are aligned with broader policy and planning strategies. Over time, climate adaptation projects should become a larger and more mainstreamed part of most country programs, with more clients requesting solutions to climate-influenced issues. While NBS have many advantages relative to hard infrastructure in the face of climate change, natural systems are also much more sensitive to climate impacts than built structures. As a result, ADB staff should be prepared to consider how NBS may interact with climate impacts, even if the primary purpose of the project does not emphasize climate adaptation.

6. Aligning Disaster Risk Management and Nature-Based Solutions at National Levels

DRM investments are an important and longstanding component of ADB programs. They often have a strong component addressing natural climate variability and extreme weather events. As with climate risks and climate adaptation, ADB has well-defined programs and methodologies to track DRM investments.

As suggested above, DRM investments typically have a strong climate adaptation component, and NBS have been widely used as part of the range of solutions to help address issues such as riparian flooding, tropical cyclone storm surges, and glacial lake outburst floods. At a CPS level, DRM and NBS can be strong complements for the full range of extreme events, including both slow-onset (drought, sea level rise, coastal erosion) and fast-onset (flooding, typhoons) events.

At a high strategic level, the role of disasters and NBS may be indirect, depending on the ADB partners and clients involved. An agriculture ministry, for instance, may have core understanding of aquifer storage and recharge as a tool for reducing drought hazards. But a more traditional DRM agency may focus more on disaster recovery, rebuilding, or short-term interventions rather than on preparation, with a much lower level of awareness of how NBS can reduce risks to begin with or how to build back better. Thus, there may be challenges.

Global, national, and regional policy initiatives may also be relevant at the CPS level. The Global Facility for Disaster Reduction and Recovery, for instance, is a knowledge and capacity building organization co-chaired by the World Bank with members such as the United Nations Office for Disaster Risk Reduction, the European

Union, and the United Nations Development Programme. The Global Platform for Disaster Risk Reduction has a similar group of partners, and it hosts both regional and global conferences that look at emerging issues and responses to DRM. NBS are a widespread and viable option and have been embraced by many in the DRM community, particularly for buffering the impact of extreme events. Many national-level agencies and multilateral development banks that coordinate DRM participate in both the Global Facility for Disaster Reduction and Recovery and the Global Platform for Disaster Risk Reduction in processes and meetings.

Although the interaction between disasters and climate change is almost universally acknowledged, agencies and NGOs that focus on DRM are, in many cases, just beginning to grapple with the implications of DRM as a type of climate adaptation. Hazard assessment for the DRM community, for instance, often remains retrospective in orientation, rather than trying to determine how climate-related disasters may evolve or shift in frequency, form, and intensity in the future, even with groups such as the United Nations World Meteorological Organization. Climate change remains an emerging issue in the Global Facility for Disaster Reduction and Recovery sessions but can be expected to grow. Many DRM agencies and organizations have only recently begun to reconsider their policies and practices from a climate adaptation perspective. The Association of Southeast Asian Nations formed a task force in 2017 to look at synergies in both risks and new policies between CCA and DRM.

Similar observations can be made for the High-Level Experts and Leaders Panel on Water and Disasters (HELP), which is chaired by the Republic of Korea as of 2020. It includes vice chairs from Indonesia and the Netherlands. Particularly for Asia and the Pacific, HELP has mobilized content and capacity, and supported new policies around water-related DRM for about 2 decades, especially for floods.

As of 2020, the coronavirus disease (COVID-19) has been redefined as a water-related disaster, and HELP has begun to explore interactions between DRM and climate change, and how NBS can help prepare for and buffer future disasters. Definitions of resilience, disasters, and recovery approaches within HELP and senior members have moved in nontraditional directions. HELP has a strong influence on the policies and best practices of many Asia and Pacific countries around DRM, and ADB plays a significant role in formulating HELP policies and statements.

V Moving Downstream: Developing Projects with Nature-Based Solutions

1. Creating Opportunities for Nature-Based Solutions: Following ADB Decision-Making Cycles

This chapter builds on Chapter 4's development of national and programmatic scale priority areas and how documents such as the ADB country partnership strategy (CPS) can help align and embed nature-based solutions (NBS) within other policy instruments. Ultimately, these high-level processes must devolve to projects. Chapter 5, therefore, focuses on the ADB project and technical assistance (TA) decision-making cycles.

The project cycle typically begins with a client approaching ADB staff with a need or problem to be addressed through a partnership, such as through TA and/or a financing process. The ADB project cycle is illustrated in Figure 5. These cycles are complementary, with TA interventions designed to support ADB project officers in implementing the overall project cycle. Realistically, the TA cycle becomes a critical component of implementing the overall project cycle specially for large projects. The two aspects cannot clearly be separated.

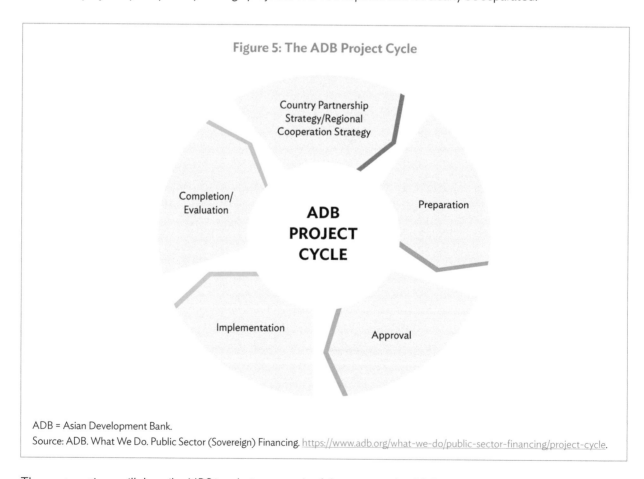

Figure 5: The ADB Project Cycle

ADB = Asian Development Bank.
Source: ADB. What We Do. Public Sector (Sovereign) Financing. https://www.adb.org/what-we-do/public-sector-financing/project-cycle.

The next sections will describe NBS in relation to each of the steps in the ADB project cycle.

2.   Country Partnership Strategy

Although discussed in more detail in Chapter 4, the CPS is a mechanism for defining a range of problems and a potential scope of strategic solutions. The CPS is a tool that can introduce NBS into discussions with clients. Upstream ADB processes, as described in Chapter 4, can make NBS easier or harder to develop and implement at the project scale. In the end, however, ADB staff will always need to follow the project cycle to develop, sort through, and evaluate potential solutions. This chapter will explore how to develop greener projects.

As a negotiated document, the CPS can ensure that a range of ADB and client staff share common values and goals, including how NBS may serve as a range of potential solutions. The CPS can also help identify potential gaps in knowledge and capacity about NBS and how ADB may be able to help fill or remove these gaps. Given that a CPS guides decisions over several years, the CPS can also help ensure a continuity of vision between ADB and the client country, spanning changes in staff and political processes.

In time, more CPSs and country operations business plans will encourage greener projects and NBS, in particular. But for many countries, existing country-level strategies may offer little support for greener investments. If NBS projects are not supported in these documents and the TA and/or client are interested in adding some greener components to the project, several options may be useful for the TA:

1. **Engage with partners early.**

    Raise the topic with internal and client partners as quickly as possible. Look for allies and become aware of potential opposition and concerns.

2. **Choose consultants carefully.**

    For the design stage, the choice of consultants will be critical, especially at the early stages. A good consultant can make the process much easier. Ideally, the consultant will be national and experienced, but partnership between national and international consultants can also help build long-term local and regional capacity for future NBS projects. Refer to Appendix 2 (Philippines Integrated Flood Risk Management) for an example of how to prepare a strong consultant terms of reference focused on NBS capacity.

3. **Select funding modalities wisely.**

    Funding modalities will be a critical early choice for the team leader. For instance, results-based lending may be more effective with clients with a stronger track record on NBS (e.g., Sandhu et al. 2006). Likewise, ADB staff should consider early if a cost–benefit analysis (CBA) and/or multicriteria analysis (MCA) project justification should be pursued. The methods are good alternatives, described in more detail below.

4. **Check if the economic internal rate of return can be reduced.**

    In some CBA cases, the team leader may be able to invoke a lower economic internal rate of return (EIRR) of 6% rather than the more standard 9%, especially if the case for lower EIRR is made at the preparation stage. According to ADB's project economic analysis guidelines, ADB's newly adopted minimum required EIRR is 9%. However, for social sector projects, selected poverty-targeting projects (such as rural roads and rural electrification), and projects that primarily generate environmental benefits (such as pollution control, protection of the ecosystem, flood control, and control of deforestation), the minimum required EIRR can be lowered to 6%. Ultimately, if ADB is to implement Strategy 2030, it may need to consider the reduction in discount rates or at least allow flexibility around the use of discount rates.

    ADB's Environment, Natural Resources, and Agriculture Division already has projects or specific outputs applying the 6% discount rate. As ADB moves toward more green investment, this will hopefully become the norm. Also, other multilaterals are using lower discount rates (2%–4%) or falling discount rates. This is done so as not to discriminate against green investments where benefits come in the later stages of the project— i.e., after 20 years or more (e.g., afforestation, climate change prevention).

5. **Explore innovative financing options. Newer options such as blended finance or green bonds may also be useful for some or all aspects of the project.**

   Well-established criteria have been developed for public–private green bonds, and some parts of Asia (e.g., India, the PRC) have robust bond markets that attract global investors (e.g., ClimateBonds.net).

6. **Use feasibility studies.**

   These studies can help test big ideas, design hypotheses, and explore innovation.

7. **Search ADB's portfolio for potential hidden assets.**

   The complexity of ADB's portfolio of available resources can sometimes unintentionally hide potential assets that can help develop, explore, or expand green components of a project.

8. **Consider how some project terms and definitions may make procurement and bidding processes more challenging.**

   Factors such as the types of firms and consultants who can engage with ADB and/or client, their experience and background, relevant expertise and analytical resources, and scope of the project will have an impact. If the team leader believes that an NBS will be the most effective approach, then obtaining a formal concept agreement with the client will be essential to flesh out the project in a form that can be financed and implemented.

3.   Preparation

The preparation stage marks a transition from strategically identifying a range of potential needs and the scope of solutions to considering specific projects, including the range of solutions that may be considered for a particular client need. The preparation stage is arguably the most important stage for NBS. You create the seeds for later success and establish expectations about the pace and scope of the project. NBS often demand a broader definition of the problem than traditional gray solution to capture the range of both direct and complementary benefits.

Regarding NBS, the project preparation stage can be made easier or more challenging depending on the CPS and other upstream processes. For instance, if the CPS does not mention or support the exploration of greener solutions, then some negotiation and explicit discussion may be necessary to ensure client support of nature-based options. Technical assistance may be especially useful at the preparation stage to ensure that a viable set of solutions can be described and developed. The following are several suggested areas of attention:

1. **Negotiate for green options**

   If ADB and client staff do not immediately agree that green options should be the currrent focus, then an important discussion is to ensure that green options get to the table alongside gray solutions. This approach is essential going into a prefeasibility analysis. ADB staff who have successfully completed NBS projects have suggested several negotiation techniques that may be more broadly useful (Appendix 2). The preparation stage is also a point when the team leader must demonstrate the performance of NBS with many clients, such as the following:

   (i)   The performance of NBS is relative to a more traditional gray solution, especially one that may have been originally envisioned by the client.

   (ii)   Nationally or locally accepted definition of "green" may differ in quality and vision with what the team leader is seeking to implement (e.g., Appendix 3). Local perception of green projects may in fact be quite gray by international standards (e.g., Appendix 2).

One consideration around performance is to open the discussion early around the problem you are intending to solve. A narrowly defined problem statement will inherently favor a gray (or grayer) solution, while a broadly defined problem will tend to support the active inclusion and counting of co-benefits that can support NBS options.

This discussion will naturally lead to questions about how green to make the project (Box 2). No simple answer exists, but several strategies are worth considering fully when the project is still primarily an idea rather than firmly defined. ADB team leaders have identified a few effective options to help ensure the greenest project possible:

(i)   Expand the "solution space" or problem shed over a wider area of influence or perspective;

(ii)   Consider including capacity building with the implementing agency;

(iii)   Consider project twinning, partnerships, co-learning or knowledge exchange;

(iv)   Take study tours with the client;

(v)   Make the project politically appealing—e.g., in Viet Nam, an NBS stormwater project was designed to ensure maintenance, reinforce the level of interest and enthusiasm, and facilitate community buy-in for the facility; and

(vi)   Document the project as a knowledge project—e.g., find ADB and external partners to communicate with the community about the project.

2. Make all projects greener.

At the project concept stage, defining several key boundaries can help make any project greener:

(i)   Include a high awareness for natural resources that may be responding rapidly to climate change. Water resources, for instance, are highly likely to vary over a project life cycle in quantity, quality, timing, and form (Smith et al. 2019). Designing projects that can interact with a shifting, often uncertain environment is expected to become critical for this century.

(ii)   Ensure that the assessment scale is relatively large to understand system dynamics and interactions. For most projects, a catchment scale is appropriate, though a basin scale of awareness may be useful for either very large high-impact projects or small basins.

(iii)   If possible, evaluate efficacy at the estimated operational lifetime of the project. Most projects globally are evaluated for environmental impacts over relatively short periods, such as the finance period (e.g., 10–20 years), which can either obscure or minimize long-term impacts for investments that may be expected to operate and influence social, economic, and ecological drivers for many decades (Hallegatte et al. 2012).

3. Get a good green design.

Even with a useful feasibility study that describes the boundaries of an effective NBS, gaps can emerge with the development of a detailed engineering design. Continuity in vision is a critical component to manage as the team leader moves to the detailed engineering design. Many good ideas can be lost, and a project may suddenly look much grayer. In some cases, foresight may lead to including a budget to help with the transition to a detailed engineering design. But several team leaders within ADB have noted that some bridging finance may be necessary to help bridge gaps, such as a staff consultancy budget. If experience with the client or the country more generally is weak on NBS, some ADB team leaders have found that directly paying for a design was a more secure way to ensure continuity.

Funding facilities within ADB may also be able to help. For instance, Urban Climate Change Resilience Trust Fund grants have been used for NBS project development that included an inventory for project officers for bridging finance and for project development. Examples include New Clark City in the Philippines and Punjab Intermediate Cities Improvement Investment Project in Pakistan (which is a grant to create socially inclusive green spaces and streets).

Box 2: Shades of Green—Developing a Green Strategy

For many types of projects, the options open to a technical assistance project are relatively clear. Energy projects, for instance, can often be "greener"—but they will rarely have strong elements of nature-based solutions. A hydropower investment can include an extensive site assessment to minimize critical ecological zone impacts such as connectivity;[a] the design can be prepared to either minimize storage or to make use of existing ecosystems for water storage;[b] and the operations can be structured around an adaptive natural flow regime.[c]

At the other extreme, projects that are designed to directly address endangered species and habitats or specific protected areas will need to be very green—built infrastructure may be minimized, or at least highly modified and sensitive to the local ecological context and needs. Although the number of climate adaptation projects at the Asian Development Bank is today relatively small, these may follow a similar pattern as well, especially in situations where climate uncertainties are high and the need to remain flexible and to minimize regrets is essential.[d]

---

[a] G. Grill et al. 2019. Mapping the World's Free-Flowing Rivers. *Nature.* 569 (7755). pp. 215–221.
[b] International Hydropower Association. 2019. *Hydropower Sector Climate Resilience Guide.* London.
[c] L. N. Poff. 2018. Beyond the Natural Flow Regime? Broadening the Hydro-Ecological Foundation to Meet Environmental Flows Challenges in a Non-Stationary World. *Freshwater Biology.* 63 (8). pp. 1011 -1021.
[d] G. Mendoza. et al. 2018. *Climate Risk Informed Decision Analysis (CRIDA): Collaborative Water Resources Planning for an Uncertain Future.* Paris: UNESCO Publishing.
Source: Authors

Developing an overall NBS strategy (or potentially several at the design stage) can help narrow the range of options that is being considered with clients. One good approach may be to focus on one main strategy, as shown in Table 7, and then consider variants in the category above and below the primary focus.

Table 7: Comparison of Nature-Based Solution Strategies

Strategy	Description	Pros	Cons	Example
Full NBS— Enhancing or Restoring Existing Ecosystem	• The primary infrastructure services come from an ecosystem already in place, even if restoration or enhancement of that ecosystem is a part of the process. The notable difference between this and the next category is that the ecosystems are already in place.	• Improving existing ecosystems is often easier than trying to create a completely new system that mirrors local, more natural systems. • The spaces are often undervalued, but the process of enhancement with local stakeholders may create political and economic wins.	• Working with existing ecosystems that have been damaged or do not have clear governance and regulatory protection can be challenging. • In some cases, special agreements may be necessary to ensure that governance and enforcement for maintenance, design, and operations are effective. • Some damaged ecosystems may be limited in their ability to recover or be restored.	• Many communities have abandoned cities with high levels of pollution or modification. Restoring natural riparian functions and ecosystems can also reorient a city to its historic reference— once again facing the river and often bringing the community back; increasing tourism, fisheries, and local businesses; and meeting more traditional infrastructure needs such as flood control.

continued on next page

Table 7 continued

Strategy	Description	Pros	Cons	Example
Full NBS— Constructed/ Engineered Ecosystem	• Often highly quantitative in implementation, using an intensive management approach to an ecosystem or even, in some cases, constructing a "new" ecosystem where one has not existed before or for a long time. These projects often have a strong multipurpose, multibenefit framework.	• Very effective for larger scale projects, especially capital-intensive and high-profile projects • Effective approach for long-lived projects, more comparable to long-lived gray infrastructure	• Requires more capacity. • Building capacity and training processes are often important. • Pilots may be necessary before scaling up. • Borrowing concepts from other ecological zones (e.g., Europe) may require some ecological contextualization. • Because of all of the above, it may take longer to implement and projects may also have a longer period to reach full operational capacity.	• Managed aquifer recharge, including both active and passive recharge • Coastal and riparian restoration, especially when removing existing gray infrastructure and dechannelizing rivers • Use of wetlands for wastewater treatment • "Room for the river" flood control projects
Wildlife and Habitat Protection	• Often framed more as engagement with protected areas or working with endangered species, these projects are usually about ensuring development and do not create critical disruption with important ecosystems and species. These projects may only include a few benefits or purposes.	• Can often access specialized international support and funding, such as from the Ramsar Convention, IUCN, CBD, and the Global Environment Facility • Often quite flexible and can be an important part of a larger adaptation program	• May foster narratives of development and humans vs. wildlife and nature, if project is scaled back or canceled. • Traditional conservation approaches may confront difficult climate change adaptation components.	• Creating wildlife corridors • Adding fish ladders or removing infrastructure barriers • Creating protected areas • Creating wildlife adaptation programs
Hybrid NBS	• Often the most diverse range of projects, where ecological and gray components merge. They often include multiple purposes and co-benefit analysis.	• Typically are cost effective and with easier buy-in from otherwise cautious stakeholders. • Projects can also be quite robust and flexible, if climate adaptation is important. • Numerous successful examples can be found globally across a wide spectrum of applications.	• Some stakeholders may be reluctant or need capacity building. • Piloting may also be important to localize the project. • Green components may have some funding, design, or procurement challenges.	• Urban resilience quite commonly uses hybrid approaches with hard gray components for drains and green wetlands for absorbing and filtering flood water. • Can include broader landscape management, such as engaging with farmers to shift flows and absorption while also building flood resilience downstream.

continued on next page

Table 7 continued

Strategy	Description	Pros	Cons	Example
Greener Gray	• This approach encompasses the growing set of ways to ensure that infrastructure projects, which must be completely or largely traditional and gray, minimize ecological impacts.	• A strong body of literature and guidance is available to guide action here, often at both national and global or sector levels. • At ADB, safeguard mechanisms and criteria are often critical. For instance, hydropower has no green equivalent, and most projects are difficult to even include hybrid components.	• In some countries, safeguarding regulations may be relatively weak, which can also expose ADB investments to some reputational risk, if local regulatory guidelines are used as a ceiling instead of as a floor.	• Evaluating ecological impacts at river basin scales, over long operational periods, and for a variety of potential climate and DRM futures • Building for operational and ecological uncertainty
Gray	• This category should, in most cases, represent an outlier. Traditional gray projects typically ignored co-benefits and focused on just one or two purposes, with little or very limited environmental impact assessment.	• Few, beyond support from very traditional agencies or highly skeptical decision-makers	• Many, especially from international audiences, the media, and local stakeholders with limited access to decision-making processes	• These projects often have high political and reputational transaction costs.

ADB = Asian Development Bank, CBD = Convention on Biological Diversity, DRM = disaster risk management, IUCN = International Union for Conservation of Nature, NBS = nature-based solutions.
Source: Authors.

4. Appraisal and/or Approval

For all projects, the appraisal and/or approval stage is when a project becomes institutionally defined as a financing process. Considerations with implementation, procurement, and evaluation are especially critical here, and NBS projects or components may require special treatment. In addition, some NBS options, such as retaining and enforcing natural edge, are seen as incurring higher design cost. It may either be lower capital expenditure but higher operational expenditure, or same capital expenditure but higher operational expediture.

In many cases, governments prefer their projects to have higher capital expenditure and lower operational expenditure. This is because they may have the budget to build (e.g., by ADB financing), but they have little or limited operation and maintenance budget. This financial gap needs to be discussed and agreed upfront, and this is one of the strong reasons for resistance by both the executing and the implementing agencies.

Preparing the economic case. Cost–benefit analyses (CBAs) are critical for all infrastructure investments. For NBS, the judgment of costs and benefits is fraught with risks (e.g., Appendix 6 on Calculating Ecosystem Economic Value). Traditional CBAs are not favorable for a wide range of emerging issues, including climate adaptation and natural infrastructure. Traditional CBAs can hurt these types of projects because they define projects narrowly. Typically, there are one or two primary purposes. Furthermore, gray infrastructure can often be highly optimized to perform those limited purposes very well, often from the start of operations.

If the CBA is applied in a traditional sense, such as using higher discount rates (e.g., above 4%), failure to consider alternative green options at the design stage and shorter time frame (e.g., at 10–15 years) leads to discriminating against green infrastructure. When the CBA uses lower or falling discount rates (also called hyperbolic discounting), longer time frames, and comprehensive ecosystem services valuation, it can be a useful decision-making tool.

In contrast, NBS perform best over a spectrum of quite distinct purposes (e.g., flood defense, public park, and natural habitat restoration) and in conditions of operational uncertainty and/or when flexibility is important. This is often the case with climate adaptation projects, where less-optimized performance may be valued. NBS are also great when quantitative performance measures may be hard to define with high confidence across a wide range of variables.

Very often, NBS also have a "ramp up" period as they slowly develop peak performance over a period of months or, in some cases, years (e.g., Appendix 5). Therefore, higher discount rates will not favor such investments since future benefits will be highly discounted. For the communities where NBS are installed, powerful benefits may exist that are hard to quantify. This may include quality of life, healthier citizens from attractive green spaces, increased tourism, pride of place, and important ecosystem services such as vibrant ecosystems.

Many of these co-benefits will also be slow to accrue. Property values are likely to evolve in quite different ways for gray solutions relative to green solutions—e.g., alongside a concrete-lined storm sewer versus a wetland and stream that serve the same function. But the benefits to property values may take several years to be well-established and clear relative to the surrounding neighborhood.

As a result, reframing the economic aspects of NBS can help ensure a more holistic set of solutions remains both visible and viable throughout the project cycle. A key aspect is to consider how to define the range of primary purposes and benefits and secondary purposes and co-benefits. Tracking the secondary aspects is often essential to the overall success of a green project because these are often the attributes of a project that will most appeal to both high-level decision-makers and communities.

These secondary aspects rarely generate revenue directly even if they have significant, even overwhelming impacts on the larger community. These include changes in real estate values, benefits to specific groups such as the urban poor or women and girls, and increased economic activity. ADB staff can often identify a range of potential secondary aspects which—with planning and careful integration within the project development cycle—can be captured as data as the project is designed and implemented. These measures may not necessarily be best captured in monetary terms. Other measures may come closer to identifying concerns that are also important to decision-makers, such as shorter commute times, increased park use, or a growth in fisheries productivity.

Since using a CBA to compare the nonmonetary co-benefits of NBS can be hard, an alternative method can be used to replace or supplement an existing financial analysis. Multicriteria analysis (MCA) is an appraisal method that measures variables such as material costs, time savings, and project sustainability as well as impact to society and the environment. MCA can assess the different investment alternatives available to achieve a given set of outcomes. In cases where standard CBA or cost-effectiveness analysis is not possible or is inadequate, MCA helps to decide the most preferred option among investment alternatives with clearly laid-out criteria and transparency.[6] MCA can also be four-pronged: environmental, social, economic, and cultural criteria. This is important particularly in places where cultural issues are very sensitive, such as the different places in the PRC.

---

[6]   For more details on MCA in the context of project economic analysis, see European Investment Bank. 2013. *The Economic Appraisal of Investment Projects at the EIB*. Luxembourg. https://www.eib.org/attachments/thematic/economic_appraisal_of_investment_projects_en.pdf; and European Commission. 2014. *Guide to Cost–Benefit Analysis of Investment Projects*. Brussels.

Unlike CBAs, MCAs are qualitative. MCAs are more rigid than informal judgments because the use of judgment criteria forces the decision-maker to compare the options. While there are several MCA approaches that can be used, they widely involve the use of a performance matrix, scoring, and weighting. In general, the approach selected depends on the desired results and level of analysis. While they can be used by themselves, MCAs are most frequently used as a complement to CBAs in considering NBS options, which allow for a comprehensive comparison of proposed NBS interventions, including monetary impacts with other nonmonetary benefits (Department for Communities and Local Government 2009).

For example, in the Philippines, a study was conducted applying a natural river management approach to identify NBS for flood risk management in six river basins. Natural river management is a way to tap natural functions of river systems to deliver climate resilience while minimizing unintended environmental and social impacts at a lower cost (ADB 2021; Penning 2020). NBS and nonstructural measures are seen to be vital for dealing with current and future environmental threats. It was indicated in the study that suitable NBS selection is highly dependent on the context and specific factors of the basin, such as the type of flooding, inhabitants, and state of the river. Although NBS upstream interventions were preferred, it was not always feasible due to hydrologic and geographic concerns.

To prioritize appropriate NBS recommendations for the select river basins, CBA and MCA were jointly applied to capture both monetary and intrinsic values in decision-making. This approach also allowed stakeholder and expert engagement through the criteria selection process, which is essential to obtain a more complete list of impacts. MCA executed in the river basins indicated that a more comprehensive list of indicators, representing multiple co-benefits, could lead to different outcomes compared to those that purely focused on monetary values under the CBA.

5.   Implementation

Implementing a project is often an intensive part of the TA cycle. It is critical to choose appropriate consultants who can support it and ensure that the original vision for NBS can be delivered. During the process, projects that have been defined with key green components may turn into much grayer projects. Because of this, strong oversight with TA may be important to ensure continuity. New gaps regarding understanding of NBS and capacity may emerge at this stage.

It is important to note that, during the appraisal and approval stages, everything is deemed ideal. In reality, numerous challenges will emerge during implementation. For example, at the feasibility and/or appraisal stages, counterparts tend to agree on the concept because of various benefits. There is also political acceptance and willingness to move forward at the appraisal stage (e.g., loan fact-finding mission). This is because, in many cases, the executing and the implementing agencies face time pressure to approve a project. However, at the detailed design and actual implementation stages, it is likely to face internal resistance, especially when the NBS concept is relatively new.

There is also often a pitfall in thinking that if the project is approved, all concepts will be applied and constructed in the field. This is not always the case. When it comes to detailed design and bidding document preparation stage, many agreed concepts are compromised to push through internal approval process and engineering reviews. Practitioners need to review and check if the intended design concept is translated and reflected into the approved bidding design and bidding documents. For example, in an ADB-supported project in Viet Nam, one of the obstacles is the design review process. The national engineering design standard promotes protecting embankment by concrete and not natural edge. It was also indicated that keeping a natural edge will encourage people to illegally encroach the area, which is not ideal.

There are also circumstances where there are changes in management or designated personnel in between processing and implementation stages. Even though previous agreements had been made on applying NBS concepts, the idea may not be fully transferred to the new management or personnel. Those newly appointed in implementation (administration) of the project will also be under a pressure of prescribed contract awards and disbursement targets. Loan covenants are also one of the instruments to ensure; however, enough attention during the implementation stage should be provided to ensure originally intended NBS concepts will be constructed in the field.

The role of construction management and supervision is also important. Construction of NBS concept requires experience. If a project management and construction supervision consultant hired under the project has no or little experience, it is likely that the quality of construction is not up to the standard; therefore, the NBS benefits will be significantly compromised.

Assess ecosystem status, conditions, and services. When developing NBS with the project team, a clear sense of the condition and relevant performance metrics of an ecosystem and/or set of NBS interventions is extremely important. A technical analysis of early components of the design stage will require data and evaluation criteria. In many countries, data may be limited, politically sensitive, not very reliable or credible, or only describe variables of interest via proxy. Several sources may be useful:

(i)   ADB environmental safeguard screens can help point out important categories of interest;

(ii)   ADB Climate Compendium, World Bank Climate Portal;

(iii) Obtaining new data via local partners, remote sensing, environmental organizations, and tools; and

(iv)   Existing ADB assessment methodologies.

Regarding climate resilience, new frameworks are emerging to understand how to manage ecosystems and natural assets for climate resilience, in general. Table 8 describes some of the main ecological resilience variables and useful categories of relevant data in more traditional infrastructure language. The emerging resilience indicators presented in the table may also be relevant, in some cases, to terrestrial and marine ecosystems.

Table 8: Resilience Principles and Emerging Resilience Indicators for Managing Freshwater Ecosystems

Resilience Principle	Resilience Indicator	Example of Resilience Metrics
Manage for Temporal Variability	• Flow and water-level regimes • Water quality regimes • Sediment regimes	• Flow metrics from indicators of hydrologic alteration, flow anomalies, water surface elevation variation • Seasonal and subseasonal variation in water quality parameters (temperature, conductivity, total nitrogen, total phosphorus) • Sedimentation rate, seasonal and subseasonal variation in total suspended solids
Manage for Spatial Heterogeneity	• Landscape heterogeneity • Floodplain inundation diversity • Physical habitat diversity and complexity	• Diversity, redundancy, and connectivity of habitat patches • Flood regime typology and delineation • River channel complexity index, shoreline complexity index, Simpson's index of diversity
Manage for Hydrologic Connectivity	• Longitudinal connectivity • Lateral connectivity	• River connectivity index, connectivity status index • Hydrologic connectivity index, proportion of floodplain connected to channel
Manage for Implementation at Basin Scales	• Basin management institutions and governance frameworks • Basin-scale water availability and supply accounting • Robust environmental monitoring systems	• Basin-scale authorities, planning processes • Spatially distributed monitoring networks to measure flow, temperature, pollutants, biotic assemblages, non-native species

Source: Adapted from T. Grantham, J. Matthews, and B. Bledsoe. 2019. Shifting Currents: Managing Freshwater Systems for Ecological Resilience in a Changing Climate. *Water Security*. 8 (Article 100049). https://doi.org/10.1016/j.wasec.2019.100049.

Climate resilience is an emerging area, with wide variations in definition and approach. In many cases, traditional resource management monitoring and evaluation metrics may not capture or accurately measure resilience as a quality that needs to be actively cultivated and managed. Several international organizations are developing resilience metrics to guide decision-making. In the case of water resources management, for instance, traditional variables largely focus on water quantity and quality. Within the past 20 years, some agencies have also added the seasonal flow regime to this list (e.g., Poff et al. 2018).

These variables largely reflect a climate-stationary and human-centric approach to water sustainability rather than water resilience. However, more recent thinking suggests that ecological resilience may have profound differences from water infrastructure resilience, which reflects how ecosystems have self-adapted to climate impacts over time.

6.   Evaluation

From the perspective of both the project officer and client, evaluation should reflect a broader definition of a problem than is normally traditional to capture the range of meaningful co-benefits defined originally in the CPS and preparation phases. Ideally, the evaluation process can also identify and reinforce institutional learning by both ADB and the client country, as well as significant stakeholders. In many cases, the evaluation process can help ensure that performance metrics help encourage future NBS projects by the host country and relevant partners, fostering institutional changes to support NBS more broadly.

VI | Choosing a Greener Future

This guide draws on input from ADB staff across a wide variety of departments, divisions and sectors. Inclusion of nature-based solutions (NBS) in ADB projects has been increasing, and staff want to ensure that the institution's investments yield the best possible results. This involves working with and not against natural systems. Ideally, this publication will be the first in a series of guidance materials and the start of a mainstreaming process.

ADB is not acting alone, of course. Most ADB partners, clients, and stakeholders throughout Asia and the Pacific have also begun to move in this direction. Some have already come far, and there is a widespread sense that traditional approaches to investment and development are no longer appropriate. Emerging issues such as climate change are forcing us to rethink the range of solutions, especially when faced with uncertainties in demography, urbanization, social and political change, and climate impacts. Flexibility is likely to be a key concept for the future for all investments, and NBS have great advantages in this realm. In keeping with this approach, suggestions for future action include the following.

(i)   Celebrate NBS successes within ADB investments, both with staff and with external audiences.

(ii) Acknowledge ADB staff who pursue green approaches, even if these projects take longer or represent smaller scale investments.

(iii) Add climate resilience and ecological sustainability goals within all sector investments (e.g., through climate resilience and vulnerability assessments).

(iv) Foster a community of practice or a working group for NBS within ADB. This could include holding regular formal and informal meetings, creating mailing lists, developing library resources, and regularly engaging with a variety of sector speakers working globally in this space. In some cases, it would be helpful to find staff who can serve as focal points or resource personnel for brainstorming and project development, and to serve as calm voices in difficult times.

(v)   Consider developing a library of state-of-the-art ADB documents that highlight NBS. This might include NBS-friendly CPS and project designs, knowledge products, and a database of NBS projects and experts.

(vi) Ensure that consultants and key agencies and NGO partners are included in the development of this area of work. ADB can be a powerful vehicle for shared learning.

(vii) Consider developing a database of consultants with NBS experience in Asia and the Pacific covering both national and international levels.

(viii) Look for closer alignment between NBS priorities and environmental safeguards, disaster risk management, and climate change adaptation.

(ix) Consider how finance mechanisms may be better aligned with NBS, such as the use of green bonds in middle-income countries, which may also serve to attract both public and private sources of finance.

(x)   Look for specific ADB processes that may inadvertently favor traditional gray investments over NBS, such as cost–benefit analyses relative to multicriteria analyses or the rules within existing procurement processes.

(xi) Help showcase examples of excellence for NBS at global and regional policy levels, and help foster new standards, criteria, and—more broadly—enabling conditions.

(xii) Work with peer multilateral development banks to accrue and build shared, complementary knowledge about what works and how to mobilize available evidence and knowledge around NBS.

In all cases, ADB is clearly making a larger transition, considering the very role and definition of infrastructure and how the bank's investments interact with natural systems over longer timescales. These shifts are part of a broader reorientation within the region and globally, and they mark an important change in how ADB works internally and with partners and clients.

1 People's Republic of China: Sponge City Designs in the Jiangxi Pingxiang Integrated Rural–Urban Infrastructure Development

Situation

Flood risk reduction is a top priority in Pingxiang, People's Republic of China. Flood frequency and severity have increased significantly since 1998. Floods in 1998, 2001, 2002, 2010, and 2014 affected more than 496,000 people, caused the collapse of more than 2,600 houses, and resulted in significant economic losses in agriculture. A major flood on 25 May 2014 severely impacted public safety and health and caused an estimated $115 million in economic losses. Most riverbanks in Pingxiang have inadequate flood protection; sediment accumulation from riverbank erosion and mining has raised riverbeds, further reducing the flood discharge capacity of rivers.

During the rainy season in April–June, flood events have a duration of several days. Water levels rise by up to 4.0 meters above normal levels for a 20-year flood (one that is likely to occur once every 20 years).

Pingxiang is a headwater municipality. All its rivers originate in the mountainous areas and flow into two river systems: (i) the Gan River, which drains northeast into Poyang Lake; and (ii) the Xiang River, which flows northwest into Dongting Lake. Where rivers flow through farmland, settlements, and industrial and mining areas they collect pollutants and sediments. At the end of 2012, the urban wastewater treatment rate in Pingxiang was 75.8%, well below the national average of 82.3%. Many small cities and townships lack or have incomplete sewer systems, and no wastewater treatment plants. Domestic wastewater is discharged untreated into rivers, affecting downstream jurisdictions and Poyang Lake. Illegal solid waste disposal along rivers is common, particularly in rural areas without regular collection. Some rivers in Pingxiang provide drinking water for local communities, and pollution poses serious risks to public health.

Action

Flood risk and the need for river rehabilitation has been identified as key development objectives for this project; hence, much attention was given to the integrated river rehabilitation and flood risk management component and subcomponents (the river projects). The design principles that the Asian Development Bank (ADB) and the project preparatory technical assistance (TA) team have been promoting to the local government and the Local Design Institute (LDI) are based on creating ecological rivers as green infrastructure as opposed to gray infrastructure, relying on traditional hardened channels for flood control.[1]

Flood safety is undoubtedly the top priority of the component but can be achieved without building high flood walls along the rivers. Instead, more space should be provided to the rivers to allow for natural seasonal fluctuations in water level. Previous ecological materials and vegetation should be used, where possible, along the riverbanks, and vegetative coverage should be maximized. Land should be provided along the rivers to allow for flood storage and detention. These measures will not only effectively reduce flood peak elevations, but also protect water quality in the river.

---

[1]   ADB. 2015. *People's Republic of China: Jiangxi Pingxiang Integrated Rural-Urban Infrastructure Development—Final Report: Main Report and Appendixes.* Consultant's report. Manila (TA 8451-PRC).

The ADB project will contribute, with the river-related infrastructure to Pingxiang's pilot as an overall strategy, by piloting sponge city design principles and green infrastructure development in the four key subcenters and the respective river areas of influence of Pingxiang Municipality in Xiangdong District urban center, Lianhua County (county seat), Luxi County (county seat), and Shangli County (county seat and Tongmu township). The ADB-funded infrastructure components have a holistic approach to sponge city infrastructure design. The integrated river rehabilitation and sustainable flood risk management components have various features and water management functions including green embankments, publicly accessible river greenways, floodplain protection, wetlands rehabilitation, and wetland parks for stormwater retention, as well as the sewer pipe component of freeing up the drainage pipes to be exclusively used for rainwater runoff.

Climate Risk Assessment Conducted

Initial climate risk screening determined that the project is at medium risk from climate change effects. A project-level climate risk and vulnerability assessment confirmed that design assumptions for flood control works were adequate. River embankments have a safety buffer freeboard of 0.5–0.7 meters that can accommodate projected increases in precipitation resulting from climate change until at least 2050.

Ecological and River Rehabilitation Assessments

Since the river projects are a significant component of the entire project, ecological and river rehabilitation specialists from AECOM were added to the project preparatory TA team after the inception mission (variation order of which was approved on 20 August 2014) to assist with the design of the integrated river rehabilitation and sustainable flood risk management components.

During the interim stage, the specialists

(i)   conducted two detailed site visits to evaluate and analyze the existing riverbank conditions, flora and fauna, landscaping, and pollution sources;

(ii)   proposed strategies for riverbank morphology design, revetment or embankment technologies, and shoreline vegetation based on existing conditions and the LDI's hydrologic calculations;

(iii) performed preliminary designs for typical nodes (river sections), including layout plan and section drawings; and

(iv) reviewed the LDI's draft feasibility study reports and provided recommendations for improving the design.

Biodiversity Study Conducted

Performing biodiversity and habitat surveys in any project area is an important first step toward biodiversity conservation. A literature review was first conducted to understand the natural conditions in Pingxiang and the possible flora and fauna in the project area. On this basis, a survey form was then developed targeting the characteristics of the survey objectives.

The survey scope and line were determined based on the available literature, satellite imagery, and information provided by the executing agency. Key sampling points for the biodiversity and habitat survey were decided according to actual conditions on site. The sample line method was used primarily for the site survey, using handheld global positioning system monitor to record the sampling route and the coordinates of sampling points. Digital cameras were used to photograph species and habitats. Communications with local residents were also recorded. At the same time, habitat conditions and species identified were recorded during the site survey. Several plant species commonly seen during the site surveys are effective in soil and water erosion protection, can provide habitat or food for animals, and are aesthetically pleasing. These plants are recommended for use in ecological rehabilitation projects in the area.

From fauna survey: These species are somewhat indicative of habitat health. Habitats suitable for them are also suitable for a variety of other organisms. The habitat requirements of these animals can be used to inform habitat optimization and development in river rehabilitation projects. This will improve protection of the species, and also provide an improved habitat environment for more organisms, increasing the ecological value of the project.

Habitat survey results: The habitat survey methodology involved combining the analysis of satellite imagery with site observations and surveys. Ten habitat types were identified in the survey area.

Capacity Building: A Critical Need

ADB project officer Stefan Rau conducted a training session to the government in August 2013 on principles of ecological river rehabilitation and flood risk management, showing benefits of the integrated and ecological approach using international state-of-the-art project cases. Rau arranged training sessions by the TA phase 1 consultants over a 2-week period in February 2014, which were held in Luxi County, with participation of the project management office as well as concerned officials from the Pingxiang municipal, county, and district governments.

2 Philippines: Integrated Flood Risk Management

The Philippines has frequently suffered from annual flooding and landslides mainly caused by typhoons, while the government has continuously strived to mitigate the damages. Such disasters have brought heavy losses to the country's economy and claimed hundreds of lives every year. Approximately 700 lives have been lost and damages have amounted to ₱8.1 billion annually.[1]

Flood control civil works have been the primary focus of flood risk management. These emphasize evacuating flood water as quickly as possible or storing it temporarily by building dikes, floodways, and reservoirs. However, it is increasingly recognized that flood control infrastructure alone is not the best flood risk management approach. They cannot completely prevent flooding, may create inequalities, contribute to ecological degradation, and may be inflexible. Hence, there needs to be basinwide flood protection infrastructure to protect the population up to a certain level of safety to ensure equality.

However, infrastructure protection alone is not adequate. There is no such thing as absolute protection. Extreme events may also lead to failure of flood protection infrastructure, which could result in devastating damages. Therefore, more comprehensive approaches that integrate flood prevention and mitigation with flood preparedness and combining structural and nonstructural measures, including more nature-based approaches, are needed.

A more comprehensive and integrated approach, taking a basinwide or catchment perspective, that may include nature-based and other soft approaches to maximize net benefits from the use of floodplains is rapidly gaining acceptance among flood management professionals. Such approach incorporates social, economic, financial, environmental, legal, and institutional aspects, as well as engineering and emergency response requirements.[2]

The Integrated Flood Risk Management Sector Project has been proposed to assist the Government of the Philippines to reduce flood risks in six river basins (Apayao–Abulog and Abra in Luzon; Jalaur in Visayas; and Agus, Buayan–Malungon, and Tagum–Libuganon in Mindanao) by (i) improving flood risk management planning through strengthening data acquisition and data management, and improving flood protection asset management; (ii) rehabilitating and constructing flood protection infrastructure; and (iii) raising community awareness and mainstreaming flood risk reduction in community development and disaster management plans to reduce the vulnerabilities of different groups. The project adopts the flood risk management strategy that aims to reduce flood risks through whole-of-river-basin approach by combining structural and nonstructural measures and integrating nature-based solutions (NBS) wherever possible and feasible.

For the preparation of the project, the Asian Development Bank (ADB) sought several international consultants with experience in NBS for flood risk management. Their terms of reference emphasized NBS components. ADB's Sustainable Development and Climate Change Department also mobilized consultants during the early stage of project preparation to recommend potential NBS that could be incorporated into the design of flood protection infrastructure.

---

[1]   CTI Engineering Co. Ltd 2004. *The Study on Flood Control Project Implementation System for Principal Rivers in the Philippines.* Summary Report under the Project for Enhancement of Capabilities in Flood Control and Sabo Engineering of the Department of Public Works and Highways. Tokyo: Japan International Cooperation Agency. https://openjicareport.jica.go.jp/pdf/11775665.pdf.

[2]   Asian Development Bank. Regional: Strengthening Integrated Flood Risk Management. https://www.adb.org/projects/52014-001/main.

3 South Asia Subregional Economic Cooperation Roads Improvement Program (Nepal) and Chittagong–Cox's Bazar Railway Project (Bangladesh)

The proposed South Asia Subregional Economic Cooperation (SASEC) Road Improvement Program (SRIP) is undertaking two strategic high-priority roads in Nepal.[1] The project roads are (i) Narayanghat–Butwal Road (115 kilometers of four-lane highway), and (ii) Bhairahawa–Lumbini–Taulihawa Road (41.13 kilometers). The project has been categorized A in accordance with the Safeguard Policy Statement (2009) of the Asian Development Bank (ADB), since one of the project components, the East West Highway Narayanghat–Butwal Section, borders the buffer zone of Chitwan National Park, covering over 23 kilometers.

Wildlife crosses the road at several points. The Bengal tiger (endangered) and greater one-horned rhinoceros (vulnerable) are protected under the National Parks and Wildlife Conservation Act of Nepal. Potential significant impacts of the Narayanghat–Butwal road will be the obstruction of wildlife movement during construction and operation.

To mitigate this risk, a minimum of five wildlife underpasses will be constructed and a biodiversity conservation plan and a compensatory afforestation program will be implemented to ensure that there are no measurable adverse impacts, no net loss of biodiversity, and that all lesser impacts are mitigated.

The Bangladesh Railway Project will pass through eight *upazilas* (subdistricts) in the Chittagong Division.[2] This project was classified (i) Category *Red* by the Department of Environment, requiring a full environmental impact assessment (EIA); and (ii) category A by ADB, also requiring a full EIA. The construction of the proposed project will take about 5 years to complete. The project will lead to permanent environmental changes to the area's topography, surface drainage pattern, air quality, and noise conditions. It will also establish a land barrier across which local farmers, wildlife, and livestock will have to become accustomed to.

The rail line passes through mostly the buffer and impact zones of three protected areas for a total length of about 29 kilometers. The three protected areas are the Chunati Wildlife Sanctuary (CWS), the Fasiakhali Wildlife Sanctuary (FWS), and the Methakatchapia National Park. Consultations with the management of these protected areas have been carried out during project preparation. The forestry officials support the project but would like the project to include proper elephant mitigation, such as overpasses or underpasses.

The rail line will cross five active elephant travel routes and six seasonal routes. Three of the active crossing points fall inside the CWS and two inside the FWS. The Asian elephant (*Elephas maximus*) is an endangered species under the red list of the International Union for Conservation of Nature and, as such, Bangladesh Railway undertook practical yet robust mitigation measures to avoid impacts on this species. These were the following:

---

[1]   Asian Development Bank (ADB). 2016. *Report and Recommendation of the President to the Board of Directors for the Proposed Loan to Nepal for the South Asia Subregional Economic Cooperation Roads Improvement Project*. Manila. https://www.adb.org/sites/default/files/project-document/210611/48337-002-rrp.pdf.

[2]   ADB. Bangladesh: SASEC Railway Connectivity Investment Program. https://www.adb.org/projects/46452-001/main.

(i)   Based on a detailed review of options, three different types of cameras plus signaling system options to help early detection of elephant presence near the rail line will be pilot tested during the first 2 years of the construction period. The pilot testing period will be used to optimize and fine-tune parameters such as speed restrictions, type of cameras, portability of the cameras, line of sight, raising awareness, procedures for operation of the system, and other factors. Based on the results of the pilot program, the respective camera option will be selected and implemented during the start of train operations.

(ii)   In addition, overpasses will be built at the active elephant crossing points. Preliminary designs, concept drawings, and costs have been prepared for the overpasses. Estimated cost for each overpass is about $3 million. An elephant awareness program will be provided to the Bangladesh Railway staff working on the section. Elephant crossings and related signs will also be erected along the line at crossing locations to alert train operators and maintenance staff.

Both projects encountered, at the early stage, a lack of appreciation for the need for wildlife crossings, specially from the engineers of the implementing agency. To address this situation, awareness programs were initiated by ADB, which included a benchmarking, training, and exposure program in Australia where key personnel (including the engineers) from the implementing agency were exposed to wildlife crossings and fully appreciated their necessity.

Another key lesson was the importance of getting the engineers, ecologists, and wildlife experts to work together on a project like this. While design of crossings was based on established guides, ecologists provide additional inputs during the design.

4 Viet Nam: Green Cities Development Project

The Secondary Green Cities Development Project (Green Cities) will develop small-scale, green, and climate resilient infrastructure in the cities of Hue, Ha Giang, and Vinh Yen in Viet Nam to strengthen socioeconomic development in the three urban areas. The project was designed in support of the green cities action plans that have been developed for each city by the Asian Development Bank (ADB) technical assistance, Green Cities: A Sustainable Urban Future in Southeast Asia (TA 8314-REG), as part of the Integrated Urban Development in Southeast Asia. Climate change resilience is explicit in the subproject designs because of the strong sensitivities of the three cities to existing climate and weather extremes. With ADB assistance, Hue City and Thua Thien Hue Province formulated a green city action plan.[1]

Based on the plan, the government and ADB further discussed Hue's green city approach. In the government's original designs, rivers and ponds would have concrete embankments rather than riprap or natural edge treatments that can support habitat for wildlife and aquatic animals. These approaches were quite new to the local partners and, in their view, rural and untidy. The government's design was not "green" by ADB standards or the latest practices in water-sensitive design.

Project officers endeavored to make changes to the project, especially on significant components that would have impact. A consulting firm, Ramboll Studio Dreiseitl (an experienced Danish company and the team that had worked on the famous Bishan Park in Singapore), was brought in to introduce water-sensitive urban design and propose changes to some project components. These included embankment design, leaving the natural edge, observation decks to provide people access to the waterfront, and circulation of water in the ponds through water pumps.

To gain acceptance for the design changes, the project officers and Thua Thien Hue project management office, led by the Department of Planning and Investment, consulted with and presented the concept to the provincial leader to gain his support. A multistakeholder consultation workshop was organized with various departments (e.g., Department of Construction, Hue Monument Conservation Center, Department of Agriculture and Rural Development). The United Nations Educational, Scientific and Cultural Organization (UNESCO) was also on board to consult with finalizing the design.[2]

The project also arranged, with the assistance of the Global Environment Facility-funded technical assistance component, to bring senior decision-makers in the project cities to Singapore for a study tour of water-sensitive design implementations in the city state. Apart from Bishan Park, the study tour visited the Punggol Waterway ridges (water-sensitive infrastructure), Kampung Admiralty (a green design building), and Jurong Lake Gardens (green landscaping). Also supported by the Global Environment Facility-funded component, an economic study that intends to show the benefits of the water-sensitive urban design green design is currently being prepared to further improve client understanding and acceptance of the nature-based design components.

1   ADB. 2015. *Hue GrEEEn City Action Plan*. Manila. https://www.adb.org/sites/default/files/publication/179170/hue-greeen-city-ap.pdf.
2   UNESCO was involved because of ADB's work inside the Hue Citadel, a UNESCO World Heritage Site.

5 People's Republic of China: Yangtze River Green Ecological Corridor Comprehensive Agriculture Development Project

The Yangtze River Green Ecological Corridor Comprehensive Agriculture Development Project will implement agriculture packages that intend to transform the existing high-input system into more productive, sustainable, and green systems; address waste issues; and promote protection and rehabilitation of agro-ecosystems.

Targeted nature-based solutions (NBS) measures were adopted across the various agriculture production bases. For example, in rice cultivation, the focus was on practices that reduce water, fertilizer and pesticide use, and greenhouse gas emissions. Adoption of water scheduling that provided water based on crop need, and balanced fertilizer application, including use of organic fertilizer and organic soil conditioners, all help to improve productivity and reduce greenhouse gas emissions.

Additionally, adoption of integrated pest management practices can help reduce the use of pesticides. To support the implementation of the activities, the project also included service centers to function as specialized extension agencies where farmers can submit soil and plant samples to be sent for testing and, based on analytical results, receive fertilizer use recommendations as well as guidance on integrated pest management.

Interest and adoption of these NBS measures at the activity level were supported as the practices are based on good agricultural practices. In consideration of the larger picture, food safety, pollution management, and protection of natural resources, this was more challenging and required considerable discussion to convey their importance beyond a cost issue and to appreciate the value of the ecological or natural approach.

To overcome this challenge, during the project development process, specialists from the Asian Development Bank and national experts were brought in to lead awareness-raising sessions on key topics such as climate smart agriculture, watershed management, and integrated river basin management. These presentations and opportunities for discussion helped to open the door to new approaches that could be adopted in the project.

To justify these new approaches, one of the serious challenges the project faced was to assign value to the co-benefits that could be derived from the NBS measures. To increase productivity and sustainability, the project expected some challenges in the short term while systems were in transition. But, over the long term, it would create more sustainable and stable production systems. The challenge was to be able to adequately quantify these benefits over the long term to justify their investment now.

Lessons Learned

1. The agriculture sector is very much reliant on natural resources. For sustainability, include NBS at the core of the work.

2. There is more work to do to quantify and understand the benefits from projects that work with natural resources and apply NBS. This will help to properly value and assign importance to these types of projects as priority investment areas.

3. Greater support is needed throughout the lifetime of these projects. Consider providing more support during administration to put in place the knowledge and capacity needed for these projects to be successful.

4. Providing better knowledge and awareness about the larger results of these projects, such as the impact and outcome intended that these projects could deliver, is essential. This will require a change from an output focus, such as construction of infrastructure and works, to more understanding of their intended purpose and function. This will also require more capacity building as part of our projects. Moreover, this will help better link projects to national strategy and development goals, as well as contribute to achieving the Sustainable Development Goals.

6 Calculating Ecosystem Economic Value

Understanding ecosystem economic value is important when evaluating the benefits of nature-based solutions (NBS). However, it is difficult to concretely quantify the value of an ecosystem because of the generally unmonetizable nature of the goods and services that it provides. Practitioners have struggled with this uncertain aspect of NBS planning and implementation, and researchers have documented the variable values of the ecosystems.

For example, a 2012 study found great economic variability for the ecosystem services provided by mangroves in Southeast Asia. The researchers found that the value varied based on location-specific elements, such as biological and societal factors, and that the value of a mangrove forest was unique to its specific location and could not be generalized across the entire region.[1]

Determining the added value of water-related projects can be particularly challenging due to their wide-ranging ecosystem interactions. A 2019 study by the Food and Agriculture Organization of the United Nations (FAO) found few Asian NBS economic evaluation cases, which further supports the challenging nature of placing an economic value on the ecosystem.[2] Additionally, nonanthropogenic-centered components such as biodiversity can be difficult to monetize. Nevertheless, even with these challenges, there are a few different methods than can be used by practitioners to support NBS implementation.

Traditionally, the economic value of an ecosystem is determined by its value to society through the goods and services it provides. Ecosystem goods are the products harvested and used by society such as timber, and ecosystem services are processes that support life and ecological well-being such as carbon sequestration and water purification.[3] Ecosystem services were initially included in ecosystem valuations to justify conservation and mitigation activities but have since been applied to other purposes as well.[4]

Ecosystem goods and services are monetized through considering their total economic value to society, which incorporates their use value, non-use value, and option value. Use value is the direct and indirect benefits that society receives from the ecosystem, and direct use, such as the sale of lumber, is directly determined by the markets. Wetlands, for example, can provide additional societal economic benefits, such as flood control, water treatment, agricultural benefits, and improved environment for fisheries; however, the economic value of those services is not set through market sales.[5]

Non-use value is derived from the knowledge that the ecosystem exists, that it can be passed down to future generations, and that it provides societal enjoyment (this includes bequest and existence values). Option value is the knowledge that the ecosystem will be available for use in the future, almost acting as a source of insurance.[6]

1   L. Brander et al. 2012. Ecosystem Service Values for Mangroves in Southeast Asia: A Meta-Analysis and Value Transfer Application. *Ecosystem Services*. 1 (1). pp. 62–69.
2   International Centre for Environmental Management (ICEM). 2019. *Identifying Nature-Based Solutions (NBS) and Green Infrastructure (GI) in the Agriculture Sector for More Resilient Rural Communities in Asia*. Final research report prepared for FAO. Ha Noi.
3   Economics for the Environment Consultancy (EFTEC). 2005. *The Economic, Social and Ecological Value of Ecosystem Services: A Literature Review*. London.
4   K. McAfee. 2012. Nature in the Market-World: Ecosystem Services and Inequality. *Development*. 55 (1). pp. 25–33.
5   N. F. Anisha et al. 2020. *Locking Carbon in Wetlands: Enhancing Climate Action by Including Wetlands in NDCs*. Corvallis, Oregon and Wageningen, The Netherlands: Alliance for Global Water Adaptation and Wetlands International.
6   New Economics Foundation. 2013. *Economics in Policy-Making 3: Valuing the Environment in Economic Terms*. London.

Together, these three components (use value, non-use value, and option value) determine an ecosystem's economic value. However, as only a segment of these components has a market valuation, the total value is mainly determined by societal preference and ideals (footnote 3).

Various tools have been developed to assist in the quantification of ecosystem services. One of the leading tools is Stanford University's Integrated Valuation of Ecosystem Services and Tradeoffs (InVest) model, a free tool that allows users to "map and value the goods and services from nature that sustain and fulfill human life."[7] It was specifically designed for decision-makers "to assess quantified tradeoffs associated with alternative management choices and to identify areas where investment in natural capital can enhance human development and conservation" (footnote 7).

Additionally, there are other tools that allow practitioners to geographically assess ecosystem services present for a specific location, such as the Toolkit for Ecosystem Service Site-Based Assessment (TESSA) and Artificial Intelligence for Ecosystem Services (ARIES). But these two are limited in that they do not provide a monetized output for the ecosystem; they only present at a particular site. However, they can be useful as a supplement to InVEST or other models.

While models do exist and are used in the Asian Development Bank (ADB), the results they produce should be utilized as an entry point into an economic assessment of an ecosystem, not as the final result. Table A6 describes three economic valuation methods for environmental goods commonly used in ADB.[8] These models inform decision-making and justify the allocation of limited resources between competing uses.

Table A6: Models of Economic Valuation Methods for Environmental Goods

Model	Description
Benefit Transfer (Value transfer and Function transfer)	Benefits transfer is another useful valuation approach that involves the adaptation and generalization of information from existing research to a different setting.[a,b] Existing primary research and studies are referred to as study cases/sites, while the setting in which the information is adapted is termed the policy case/site. The policy site may differ from the study sites in terms of economic, biophysical, temporal, and/or spatial situations.[c,d]
Contingent Valuation	In the 1989 Exxon Valdez incident, the contingent valuation method was validated by the United States government and judicial systems to assess the environmental damage of the oil spill and its impacts on beaches, coasts, and wildlife habitats. The contingent valuation method has since become the most common and widely adopted environmental valuation method in the literature.
Choice Modeling	Choice modeling uses comparisons among alternative options to examine preferences in the context of trade-offs.[e] It has many variants, including choice experiments, choice ranking, discrete choice modeling, and conjoint analysis. Choice modeling has been used for a wide range of nonmarket benefits and can be potentially employed in any context where contingent valuation is used. It is particularly useful when the intention is to understand the value of multiple attributes of a nonmarket service.

[a] A. M. Freeman. 1984. On the Tactics of Benefit Estimation under Executive Order 12291. In V. K. Smith, ed. *Environmental Policy under Reagan's Executive Order: The Role of Benefit–Cost Analysis*. Chapel Hill: The University of North Carolina Press.

[b] E. Quah and R. Toh. 2012. *Cost–Benefit Analysis: Cases and Materials*. London: Routledge.

[c] A. M. Freeman. 2003. *The Measurement of Environmental and Resource Values: Theory and Methods*. 2nd ed. Washington, DC: Resources for the Future.

[d] M. A. Wilson and J. P. Hoehn. 2006. Valuing Environmental Goods and Services Using Benefit Transfer: The State-of-the Art and Science. *Ecological Economics*. 60 (2). pp. 335–342.

[e] Asian Development Bank. 2017. *Guidelines for the Economic Analysis of Projects*. Manila.

Source: E. Quah and T. S. Tan. 2019. Valuing the Environment. *ADBI Working Paper Series*. No. 1012. Tokyo: Asian Development Bank Institute. https://www.adb.org/sites/default/files/publication/532731/adbi-wp1012.pdf.

[7] InVEST. 2020. Natural Capital Project. https://naturalcapitalproject.stanford.edu/software/invest.

[8] E. Quah and T. S. Tan. 2019. Valuing the Environment. *ADBI Working Paper Series*. No.1012. Tokyo: Asian Development Bank Institute.

A literature review conducted by the FAO showed that the existing economic assessments for NBS projects have various shortcomings (footnote 2). Therefore, practitioners and decision-makers should be wary of model-produced economic evaluations and should conduct their own additional research based on their expert knowledge and experience with the ecosystem of interest.

Some economic benefits of NBS are not included in models. For example, while not an ecosystem service per se, job creation is an important added benefit of NBS and can be included in calculating the added value of an NBS project. For instance, in addition to the added climate and ecosystem benefits, Pakistan is generating approximately 60,000 jobs as part of their newly implemented sustainable forestry practices.[9] The value added from job creation would not be represented in the existing evaluating systems and would require insider knowledge to deduce.

An alternative to trying to value an ecosystem by the goods and services it produces is to try to determine the substantial avoided costs of its loss. In other words, it is never intended to value how much an entire ecosystem is worth. However, practitioners could quantify how much value will be lost by its absence because of implementing an investment. In this line of reasoning, ecosystems are not only valued for the benefits but also for the damage incurred by their absence. For example, mangroves provide flood protection. Their global absence could negatively affect up to 15 million people annually (footnote 9). The incurred costs associated with flooding and other damages can be used to support NBS. Employing this alternative approach can be useful when justifying why existing NBS or green infrastructure should be maintained, reinvested in, or favored over gray infrastructure investments.

Finally, while it is not an ecosystem evaluation tool per se, the global Reducing Emissions from Deforestation and Forest Degradation (REDD or REDD+) framework can be used to incentivize countries to implement NBS solutions relating to forest management and climate mitigation (i.e., greenhouse gas atmospheric concentrations). The framework does not provide a value for the entire ecosystem, but it does support using economic tools to motivate green infrastructure investment. This rationale can be useful when justifying NBS projects that may involve carbon-intensive ecosystems such as forests, coastal wetlands, and peatlands.

While there is no definitive method for determining exact ecosystem economic value, the methods and trains of thought presented here provide a starting point for practitioners to support the implementation of NBS and compare their potential benefits to those of gray infrastructure projects. In cases where economic value is highly difficult to quantify, practitioners could also view the ecosystem as an already existing piece of infrastructure and compare the benefits of green infrastructure elements to that of gray or hybrid infrastructure, such as in the arena of flood control or fisheries management. This comparison method could be a good starting point for evaluating a potential infrastructure project. Finally, it is worth noting that ecosystem value is elastic, and its benefits fluctuate over time; therefore, constant reevaluation of value and services provided is essential to properly understand an ecosystem and its benefits.

---

[9]   Organisation for Economic Co-operation and Development (OECD). 2020. Nature-Based Solutions for Adapting to Water-Related Climate Risks. *OECD Environmental Policy Papers.* No. 21. Paris: OECD Publishing.

References

Abell, R. et al. 2017. *Beyond the Source: The Environmental, Economic and Community Benefits of Source Water Protection*. Arlington, VA: The Nature Conservancy.

Acclimatise. 2018. *AWARE* for *Projects: Fast, Comprehensive Climate Risk Screening*. http://www.acclimatise.uk.com/wp-content/uploads/2018/11/Aware_brochure_Nov2018.pdf.

Altamirano, M. 2019.*Hybrid (Green–Gray) Water Security Strategies: A Blended Finance Approach for Implementation at Scale*. Presentation during the Roundtable on Financing Water. Regional Meeting Asia. Manila. 26–27 November. https://www.oecd.org/water/Session3b.Hybrid_(green- gray)_water_security_strategies.pdf.

Anderson, J. et al. 2019. Conservation Finance Takes Off as the Netherlands Issues One of the Largest Green Bonds Ever. Blog. World Resources Institute. https://www.wri.org/blog/2019/06/conservation-finance-takes-netherlands-issues-one-largest-green-bonds-ever.

Anisha, N. F. et al. 2020. *Locking Carbon in Wetlands: Enhancing Climate Action by Including Wetlands in NDCs*. Corvallis, Oregon and Wageningen, The Netherlands: Alliance for Global Water Adaptation and Wetlands International. https://www.wetlands.org/publications/locking-carbon-in-wetlands/.

Arup. 2014. *City Resilience Framework*. City Resilience Index. New York: The Rockefeller Foundation. https://www.arup.com/perspectives/publications/research/section/city-resilience-index.

Asian Development Bank. Bangladesh: SASEC Railway Connectivity Investment Program. https://www.adb.org/projects/46452-001/main.

———. 2016. *Report and Recommendation of the President to the Board of Directors for the Proposed Loan to Nepal for the South Asia Subregional Economic Cooperation Roads Improvement Project*. Manila. https://www.adb.org/sites/default/files/project-document/210611/48337-002-rrp.pdf.

———. 2017. *Guidelines for the Economic Analysis of Projects*. Manila. https://www.adb.org/sites/default/files/institutional-document/32256/economic-analysis-projects.pdf.

———. 2018. *Strategy 2030: Achieving a Prosperous, Inclusive, Resilient, and Sustainable Asia and the Pacific*. Manila. https://www.adb.org/sites/default/files/institutional-document/435391/strategy-2030-main-document.pdf.

———. 2020. *COVID-19 Recovery: A Pathway to a Low-Carbon and Resilient Future*. Manila. https://www.adb.org/publications/covid-19-recovery-low-carbon-resilient-future.

———. 2020. *Protecting and Investing in Natural Capital in Asia and the Pacific: A Practitioner's Guide to Nature-Based Solutions.* Consultant's report. Manila (TA 9461-REG). https://www.adb.org/sites/default/files/project-documents/50159/50159-001-tacr-en_3.pdf.

———. 2021. *Guidelines for Mainstreaming Natural River Management in Water Sector Investments.* Manila. https://www.adb.org/sites/default/files/publication/737006/guidelines-mainstreaming-natural-river-management.pdf.

Bauduceau, N. et al. 2015. *Towards an EU Research and Innovation Policy Agenda for Nature-based Solutions & Re-naturing Cities: Final Report of the Horizon 2020 Expert Group on 'Nature-based Solutions and Re-naturing Cities'.* Luxembourg: Publications Office of the European Union. https://doi.org/10.2777/765301.

Brander, L. et al. 2012. Ecosystem Service Values for Mangroves in Southeast Asia: A Meta-Analysis and Value Transfer Application. *Ecosystem Services.* 1 (1). pp. 62–69. doi: https://doi.org/10.1016/j.ecoser.2012.06.003.

Brauman, K. et al. 2019. Water Funds. In L. A. Mandle et al., eds. *Green Growth that Works.* Washington, DC: Island Press. pp.118–140. doi:10.5822/978-1-64283-004-0_9.

Bridges, T. 2015. *Use of Natural and Nature-Based Features (NNBF) for Coastal Resilience.* Vicksburg, MS: US Army Corps for Engineers, Engineer Research and Development Center. https://erdc-library.erdc.dren.mil/jspui/handle/11681/4769.

Brière, C. et al. 2018. Usability of the Climate-Resilient Nature-Based Sand Motor Pilot, The Netherlands. *Journal of Coastal Conservation.* 22 (3). pp. 491–502.

Browder, G. et al. 2019. *Integrating Green and Gray: Creating Next Generation Infrastructure.* Washington, DC: World Bank and World Resources Institute. https://files.wri.org/s3fs-public/integrating-green-gray-executive-summary.pdf.

Brown, C. et al. 2020. Resilience by Design: A Deep Uncertainty Approach for Water Systems in a Changing World. *Water Security.* 9 (Article 100051). https://doi.org/10.1016/j.wasec.2019.100051.

Climate Bonds Initiative (CBI). 2018. *Water Infrastructure Criteria under the Climate Bonds Standard: Criteria Document.* London.

Cohen-Shacham et al., eds. 2016. *Nature-based Solutions to Address Global Societal Challenges.* Gland, Switzerland: International Union for Conservation of Nature. https://portals.iucn.org/library/sites/library/files/documents/2016-036.pdf.

Cooper, R. and J. H. Matthews. 2020. Water Finance and Nature-Based Solutions. *K4D Helpdesk Report.* No. 857. Brighton, UK: Institute of Development Studies.

CTI Engineering Co. Ltd. 2004. *The Study on Flood Control Project Implementation System for Principal Rivers in the Philippines.* Summary Report under the Project for Enhancement of Capabilities in Flood Control and Sabo Engineering of the Department of Public Works and Highways. Tokyo: Japan International Cooperation Agency. https://openjicareport.jica.go.jp/pdf/11775665.pdf.

Deltacommissie. 2008. *Working Together with Water: A Living Land Builds for its Future.* Findings of the Deltacommissie. Den Haag, the Netherlands. http://www.deltacommissie.com/doc/deltareport_full.pdf.

Dillon, P. et al. 2010. Managed Aquifer Recharge: Rediscovering Nature as a Leading Edge Technology. *Water Science and Technology.* 62 (10). pp. 2338–2345. doi:10.2166/wst.2010.444.

Economics for the Environment Consultancy (EFTEC). 2005. *The Economic, Social and Ecological Value of Ecosystem Services: A Literature Review.* London. https://www.cbd.int/financial/values/unitedkingdom-valueliterature.pdf.

European Investment Bank (EIB). 2019. *Investing in Nature: Financing Conservation and Nature-Based Solutions.* Luxembourg. https://www.eib.org/attachments/pj/ncff-invest-nature-report-en.pdf.

Food and Agriculture Organization of the United Nations (FAO). 2010. *Managing Forests for Climate Change.* Rome. http://www.fao.org/3/i1960e/i1960e00.pdf.

Freeman, A. M. 1984. On the Tactics of Benefit Estimation under Executive Order 12291. In V. K. Smith, ed. *Environmental Policy under Reagan's Executive Order: The Role of Benefit–Cost Analysis.* Chapel Hill: The University of North Carolina Press.

———. 2003. *The Measurement of Environmental and Resource Values: Theory and Methods.* 2nd ed. Washington, DC: Resources for the Future.

Garcia, L. E. et al. 2014. *Beyond Downscaling: A Bottom-Up Approach to Climate Adaptation for Water Resources Management.* Washington, DC: World Bank.

Government of the United Kingdom, Department for Communities and Local Government. 2009. *Multi-Criteria Analysis: A Manual.* London. http://www.communities.gov.uk/documents/corporate/pdf/1132618.pdf.

Government of the United States, California Department of Water Resources. 2017. *FLOOD-MAR: Using Flood Water for Managed Aquifer Recharge to Support Sustainable Water Resources.* California. https://water.ca.gov/-/media/DWR-Website/Web-Pages/Programs/Flood-Management/Flood-MAR/DWR_FloodMAR-White-Paper_a_y20.pdf?la=en&hash=9D81DB6FC3DF2C20496C61FD18B1A2C8F885A98A.

Grantham, T., J. Matthews, and B. Bledsoe. 2019. Shifting Currents: Managing Freshwater Systems for Ecological Resilience in a Changing Climate. *Water Security.* 8 (Article 100049). https://doi.org/10.1016/j.wasec.2019.100049.

Grill G. et al. 2019. Mapping the World's Free-Flowing Rivers. *Nature.* 569 (7755). pp. 215–221. https://doi.org/10.1038/s41586-019-1111-9.

Hallegatte, S. et al. 2012. *Investment Decision Making Under Deep Uncertainty—Application to Climate Change.* Washington, DC: World Bank.

High-Level Experts and Leaders Panel on Water and Disasters (HELP). 2019. *HELP Global Report on Water and Disasters.* Tokyo. https://www.wateranddisaster.org/cms310261/wp-content/uploads/2019/07/HELP-Global-Report-on-Water-and-Disasters-D9-20190607_s.pdf.

Integrated Valuation of Ecosystem Services and Tradeoffs (InVEST). 2020. Natural Capital Project. https://naturalcapitalproject.stanford.edu/software/invest.

Intergovernmental Panel on Climate Change (IPCC). 2012: Glossary of Terms. In C. B. Field et al., eds. *Managing the Risks of Extreme Events and Disasters to Advance Climate Change Adaptation: A Special Report of Working Groups I and II of the Intergovernmental Panel on Climate Change.* New York: Cambridge University Press. pp. 555–564. https://archive.ipcc.ch/pdf/special-reports/srex/SREX-Annex_Glossary.pdf.

International Centre for Environmental Management (ICEM). 2019. *Identifying Nature-Based Solutions (NBS) and Green Infrastructure (GI) in the Agriculture Sector for More Resilient Rural Communities in Asia.* Final research report prepared for FAO. Ha Noi.

International Hydropower Association. 2019. *Hydropower Sector Climate Resilience Guide.* London. https://assets-global.website-files.com/5f749e4b9399c80b5e421384/5fa7e38ce92a9c6b44e63414_hydropower_sector_climate_resilience_guide.pdf.

International Union for Conservation of Nature (IUCN). 2017. *Issues Brief: Peatlands and Climate Change.* Gland, Switzerland. https://www.iucn.org/sites/dev/files/peatlands_and_climate_change_issues_brief_final.pdf.

———. 2020. Mekong WET. https://www.iucn.org/regions/asia/our-work/regional-projects/mekong-wet.

Li, X., G. Turner, and L. Jiang. 2012. *Grow in Concert with Nature: Sustaining East Asia's Water Resources through Green Water Defense.* Washington, DC: World Bank.

Lu, X. 2019. Building Resilient Infrastructure for the Future: Background Paper for the G20 Climate Sustainability Working Group. *ADB Sustainable Development Working Paper Series.* No. 61. Manila: Asian Development Bank.

Maddrell, S. and I. Neal. 2012. *Sand Dams: A Practical Guide.* London. https://www.samsamwater.com/library/Maddrell_and_Neal_2012_Sand_Dams_a_Practical_Guide_LR.pdf.

Matthews, J. et al. 2019. *Wellspring: Source Water Resilience and Climate Adaptation.* Arlington, VA: The Nature Conservancy. https://www.nature.org/content/dam/tnc/nature/en/documents/Wellspring_FULL_Report_2019.pdf.

Mayor of London. 2016. *The London Plan.* London: Greater London Authority. https://www.london.gov.uk/sites/default/files/the_london_plan_2016_jan_2017_fix.pdf.

McAfee, K. 2012. Nature in the Market-World: Ecosystem Services and Inequality. *Development.* 55 (1). pp. 25–33. DOI:10.1057/dev.2011.105.

Mendoza, G. et al. 2018. *Climate Risk Informed Decision Analysis (CRIDA): Collaborative Water Resources Planning for an Uncertain Future.* Paris: UNESCO Publishing.

Nesshöver, C. et al. 2017. The Science, Policy and Practice of Nature-Based Solutions: An Interdisciplinary Perspective. *Science of the Total Environment.* 579. pp. 1215–1227.

New Economics Foundation. 2013. *Economics in Policy-Making 3: Valuing the Environment in Economic Terms.* London. https://www.nefconsulting.com/wp-content/uploads/2014/10/Valuing-the-environment-in-economic-terms-briefing.pdf.

Ontl, T. A. and L. A. Schulte. 2012. Soil Carbon Storage. *Nature Education Knowledge.* 3 (10). p. 35.

Organisation for Economic Co-operation and Development (OECD). 2019. *Responding to Rising Seas: OECD Country Approaches to Tackling Coastal Risks.* Paris: OECD Publishing. https://doi.org/10.1787/9789264312487-en.

———. 2020. Nature-Based Solutions for Adapting to Water-Related Climate Risks. *OECD Environmental Policy Papers.* No. 21. Paris: OECD Publishing. https://doi.org/10.1787/2257873d-en.

Ozment, S., G. Ellison, and B. Jongman. 2019. *Nature-Based Solutions for Disaster Risk Management.* Washington, DC: World Bank. http://documents.worldbank.org/curated/en/253401551126252092/Booklet.

Penning, E. 2020. *Nature-Based Solutions in River Management.* PowerPoint Presentation for EurAqua. https://www.euraqua.org/download/18.b9c38d6174e52ec0a3493/1601895777489/Nature%20Based%20 Solutions%20in%20River%20Management_Penning.pdf.

Poff, L. N. 2018. Beyond the Natural Flow Regime? Broadening the Hydro-Ecological Foundation to Meet Environmental Flows Challenges in a Non-Stationary World. *Freshwater Biology.* 63 (8). pp. 1011–1021.

Poff, L. N. et al. 2016. Sustainable Water Management under Future Uncertainty With Eco-Engineering Decision Scaling. *Nature Climate Change.* 6 (1). pp. 25–34. DOI:10.1038/nclimate2765.

Quah, E. and T. S. Tan. 2019. Valuing the Environment. *ADBI Working Paper Series.* No. 1012. Tokyo: Asian Development Bank Institute. https://www.adb.org/sites/default/files/publication/532731/adbiwp1012.pdf.

Quah, E. and R. Toh. 2012. *Cost–Benefit Analysis: Cases and Materials.* London: Routledge.

Quesne, T. et al. 2010. Flowing Forward: Freshwater Ecosystem Adaptation to Climate Change in Water Resources Management and Biodiversity Conservation. *Water Working Notes.* No. 28. Washington, DC: World Bank. http://documents.worldbank.org/curated/en/953821468146057567/Flowing-forward-freshwater-ecosystem-adaptation-to-climate-change-in-water-resources-management-and-biodiversity-conservation.

Ray, P. and C. Brown. 2015. *Confronting Climate Uncertainty in Water Resources Planning and Project Design: The Decision Tree Framework.* Washington, DC: World Bank.

Raymond, C. et al. 2017. A Framework for Assessing and Implementing the Co-Benefits of Nature-Based Solutions in Urban Areas. *Environmental Science & Policy.* 77. pp. 15–24. https://doi.org/10.1016/j.envsci.2017.07.008.

Resources, Environment, and Economics Center for Studies Inc. (REECS) and Deltares. Final Report Nature-Based Solutions in Philippine River Basins. Unpublished.

Sandhu, S. C. et al. 2006. *Management of Environment and Social Issues in Highway Projects in India.* Washington, DC: World Bank.

Silva, M. et al. 2020. *Increasing Infrastructure Resilience with Nature-Based Solutions (NBS): A 12-Step Technical Guidance Document for Project Developers.* Washington, DC: Inter-American Development Bank.

Simpson, E. H. 1949. Measurement of Diversity. *Nature.* 163 (4148). p. 688. https://www.nature.com/articles/163688a0.

Smith, D. M. et al. 2019. *Adaptation's Thirst: Accelerating the Convergence of Water and Climate Action.* Background paper prepared for the 2019 report of the Global Commission on Adaptation. Rotterdam and Washington, DC.

Sutton-Grier, A., K. Wowk, and H. Bamford. 2015. Future of Our Coasts: The Potential for Natural and Hybrid Infrastructure to Enhance the Resilience of Our Coastal Communities, Economies and Ecosystems. *Environmental Science & Policy.* 51. pp. 137–148.

Timmerman, J. et al. 2017. Improving Governance in Transboundary Cooperation in Water and Climate Change Adaptation. *Water Policy*. 19 (6). pp. 1014–1029. https://doi.org/10.2166/wp.2017.156.

United Nations. 2015. *Transforming Our World: The 2030 Agenda for Sustainable Development.* https://sustainabledevelopment.un.org/post2015/transformingourworld/publication.

Water Global Practice. 2016. *Case Studies in Blended Finance for Water and Sanitation: Water Revolving Fund in the Philippines*. Washington, DC: World Bank. https://www.globalwaters.org/sites/default/files/philippines-worldbank-Blended-Finance-case-study.pdf.

Watkiss, P., R. Wilby, and C. Rodgers. 2020. Principles of Climate Risk Management for Climate Proofing Projects. *ADB Sustainable Development Working Paper Series*. No. 69. Manila: ADB. https://www.adb.org/publications/climate-risk-management-climate-proofing-projects.

Whipple, A. A., J. H. Viers, and H. E. Dahlke. 2017. Flood Regime Typology for Floodplain Ecosystem Management as Applied to the Unregulated Cosumnes River of California, United States. *Ecohydrology*. 10 (5). https://doi.org/10.1002/eco.1817.

Wilson, M. A. and J. P. Hoehn. 2006. Valuing Environmental Goods and Services Using Benefit Transfer: The State-of-the Art and Science. *Ecological Economics*. 60 (2). pp. 335–342.

World Bank. 2019a. *Building Urban Water Resilience in Small Island Countries: The Case of South Tarawa, Kiribati*. Washington, DC. https://openknowledge.worldbank.org/handle/10986/32525.

————. 2019b. *Nature-Based Solutions for Disaster Risk Management*. Washington, DC. http://documents1.worldbank.org/curated/en/253401551126252092/pdf/134847-NBS-for-DRM-booklet.pdf.

World Water Assessment Program and United Nations Water. 2018. *The United Nations World Water Development Report 2018: Nature-Based Solutions for Water*. Paris: United Nations Educational, Scientific and Cultural Organization.

WWF. 2017. *Natural and Nature-Based Flood Management: A Green Guide*. Washington, DC. https://www.worldwildlife.org/publications/natural-and-nature-based-flood-management-a-green-guide.

————. 2019. *Dutch Fund for Climate and Development*. https://wwfeu.awsassets.panda.org/downloads/dutch_climate_fund_2_pager_final.pdf.